DISCOVERING
REIGATE PRIORY

The place and the people

Audrey Ward

Bluestream Books

DISCOVERING
REIGATE PRIORY

The place and the people

First published September 1998
© Audrey Ward

ISBN: 1-901860-02-7

Published by **Bluestream Books,
1 Howard Road, Reigate, Surrey RH2 7JE
Tel: 01737 222030   Fax: 01737 240185**

Editor: Grace Filby
Associate Editor: Denis Ward
Publisher: Peter Filby
Page design: Alan English
Repro by Brooklands Publishing, Dormansland
Print by Grapevine, Sompting, West Sussex

CONTENTS

ACKNOWLEDGEMENTS

I wish to express thanks to all the people who have helped me in so many ways to discover and record the history of Reigate Priory.

Some names I never knew and some I may have forgotten, but I am most grateful to them all:

James Batley, the Duke of Beaufort, Mark Bohannon, Dr Bonwitt, Don Burgess, Carolyn Burnley, Gilly Cox, Douglas Sylvanus Davis, Mark Davison, Roger Ellaby, the Earl of Effingham, John and Barbara Ferguson, Amy Filby, Mr Gammon, Sean Hawkins, James and Sarah Hervey-Bathurst, John Janaway, Doris Ker, Noel Lellman, Ray Luff, John Macanally, James McCulloch, Frank Millard, Roger Mintey, Mrs Molyneux, Alan Moore, Peter Newland, Lynne Price, Peter Pratt, Martin Roth, Mary Saaler, Mary Slade, Vera and Ray Strank, Canon Richard Thomson, Dennis Turner, David Williams.

Eileen Wood must have a special thank-you for all the trouble she has taken to save my time and energy by making the Museum information easily accessible.

Thanks are due, too, to the staffs of:
Reigate Priory School and Museum
Aberdour House
Burghley
Cambridge County Records Office
Dingley Hall
Grantully Castle
Surrey County Records Office
Croydon Local Studies Library
Guildford Local Studies Library
The Bass Museum, Burton upon Trent
Winchester Diocesan Records Office.

N.B. The Surrey Records Office and Guildford Local Studies Library transferred their collections to Woking in the autumn of 1998.

Permission to use quotations and pictures has been kindly granted by:
The *Country Life* Picture Library
Countrywide Books and the Surrey Federation of Women's Institutes (to quote from *Surrey Within Living Memory*)
The House of Lords Library
The Royal Institute of British Architects
Surrey County Council Archaeological Unit
The Surrey Mirror, Surrey and Sussex Newspapers
Wilton House, Wilton.

A special thank-you, too, to photographer Mike Couchman, and to the contributing photographers, Cecilia Barrett, Patrick Connolly, Albert Epps and others.

Without my husband and my daughter it would have been quite impossible. Not only has Denis tirelessly word-processed my longhand, but he has shared the excitement of discovery and he has driven hundreds of miles in the hunt for clues.

Our daughter Grace has been the perfect editor, encouraging, experienced and always constructive.

Charlotte Wilson, a Priory pupil, painted the charming water-colour used on this book's cover when she was ten years old. Through her young eyes it captures the delight of discovery.

INTRODUCTION

'Please write it all down, before it is too late!'

For some years now - perhaps since my hair turned white - this has been the urgent message to me from visitors, from past pupils, from friends, from family and from people who have listened to my talks about Reigate Priory's unfolding history. So here it is - or at least some of it!

Reigate Priory is scheduled as an ancient monument, for it has a past stretching over eight centuries. It is unique in Surrey, for it is the only priory to survive as a viable building. The secret and the wonder of its survival is that it has been adapted for use by each of its owners and yet it retains some of its original structure and many of its architectural glories.

Some of its history is recorded in books and documents, some evidence remains visible in and around the building, and some is buried underground or hidden within the walls. But there is even more to be discovered and much of the evidence is scattered.

Over the years much of it has found its way home and, out of the blue, we have received maps, pictures, family trees, documents, visitors' books, sale books, letters and recorded memories. All these and many more gifts have added to our knowledge and, like pieces of a giant jigsaw puzzle, have given us a more comprehensive picture of the Priory in the past. This material is now kept in our own Priory Museum and can be made available for reference.

Since 1971 I have had the fun, not only of trying to put the jigsaw pieces together, but of hunting for more information both locally and further afield. We have met many helpful and interesting people and have made many new friends. The search has led to all sorts of unusual experiences and exciting discoveries. We found Elizabeth Howard and Humphrey Parsons at Woburn, part of a 15th century Priory seal at Cambridge, Lady Henry Somerset's little sister at Eastnor Castle, Admiral Beatty's dog at Duxford, John Grano's diary in the Bodleian Library, and a Hilliard miniature of Charles Howard in the Earl of Effingham's pocket. In books we were reading, too, there were unexpected references and connections with the Priory and its people.

And that is what this book is about - Discovering Reigate Priory.

I have had to limit the scope to the building and the people who have used it, but there are many more aspects to be explored. The park and the gardens, for instance, need a book to themselves. Their geology, archaeology, flora, fauna and human stories are surprisingly varied and interesting.

No book about the Priory can be definitive, for new information is constantly emerging, and the interpretation of our framework of facts changes accordingly.

Most of our knowledge is based on the excellent research by Ernest Scears, whose booklet - now out of print - summarised the Priory's history until 1945.

But history grows from living memories, which need to be captured and set down, so in my last two chapters I have tried to bring the written story of the Priory up to date.

I would like to thank all the people who have made this book possible. I hope they will enjoy the result.

THE AUGUSTINIAN PRIORY

*T*he time was the early 1200s. The place was the Priory of St Mary over the water (St Mary Overie) which we now know as Southwark Cathedral. Leaving through the gatehouse, first came the horses carrying the escort, discreetly armed, wearing chequered surcoats of blue and gold, and bearing the pennant of William de Warenne.

Next, riding mules, came the little group in their charge, monks wearing coarse black woollen cloaks, hitched up over their simple leather belts. As they rode out they pulled their hoods over their shining tonsured heads, bent forward, gave a little nudge with their heels and hurried to keep pace with their protectors.

Behind them they left a bustling scene of busy workmen, all hard at work repairing and rebuilding the great Priory, which had been so badly ravaged by fire. Moored on the river bank close to London Bridge there were barges laden with stone, timber, lime and sand, supplies for the restoration.

The little party turned south, first following a well worn track. Their journey was to be only twenty miles or so, but as they left in the afternoon, just after evensong, they gratefully accepted the hospitality of their Augustinian brethren at Merton, then continued early next day on their journey to Reygate. Now the way was rougher and often uphill, until suddenly the land dropped before them. They stopped on the high chalk ridge, viewing the vast panorama of trees and hills stretching for miles to the south, to the east and to the west. This was the Holmesdale, with the almost impenetrable Weald beyond.

Not far below them there were signs of habitation, wisps of smoke from cooking fires and little cultivated clearings. Raised on a mound stood the castle, flying the blue and gold chequered flag of the Warennes. Now there was

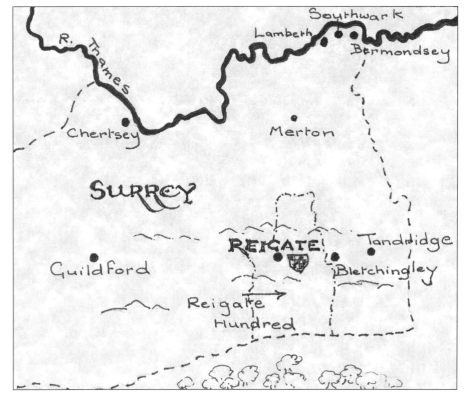

only the steep slippery chalk track to negotiate and they would reach their goal.

They hurried down into the little town, passing the castle barbican on the left. Here perhaps their escort rode back into the bailey, for the black-robed figures on their sturdy grey mules were safe now and had not far to go. 'Through the market place, past the ale-house and down the lane' were their directions. Rumbling beside them now were heavy wooden carts with solid wheels, laden with great blocks of grey local stone. Then, through the archway of the gatehouse, they could see their new half-built home, Reigate Priory.

This flight of fancy is, I admit, how my imagination clothes the few hard facts available to us.

Cherchefelle and the Warennes

Reigate Priory was founded by William de Warenne, who was the sixth Earl of Surrey from 1201 to 1240. Until recently the date has been quoted as 1235 A.D., but there is documentary evidence that it was already a priory by 1233 and archaeological evidence suggests that building

The seal of John De Warenne 1329. This picture is a rebus – a play on the family name of Warenne.

could have been started some years earlier. The family was descended from one of the chief Norman barons who in 1066 supported William of Normandy in his invasion of England. The

Reliving history at Reigate Castle. The King and Earl William de Warenne confront a de Clare rival.

Warennes established various strongholds, including those at Castle Acre in Norfolk, Wakefield and Conisbrough in Yorkshire, Stamford in Lincolnshire, Lewes in Sussex, and here at Cherchefelle in Surrey.

In the Domesday Book, William the Conqueror's inventory, Cherchefelle had been recorded as having arable land, meadowland, woodland, herds of pigs, two mills, 67 villagers and 11 smallholders. At that time it was owned by Queen Edith, widow of Edward the Confessor. Though it was small, it was important enough to give its name to one of Surrey's 14 administrative districts, the Hundred of Cherchefelle.

The name Cherchefelle could mean 'Church field' or 'hill field'. It is likely that there was an earlier church on the hill where Reigate Parish Church now stands, for part of a carved stone Saxon cross was found nearby and is now safely preserved in the vestry where the Cranston Library is housed.

The settlement had developed on lower ground to the west on the banks of the little stream - the Rie or Wray. When the site of the old vicarage in Church Street was excavated in the 1970s, archaeologists found rubbish pits, tools, spindle whorls, pottery and even a bone ice-skate.

When Queen Edith died, the second William de Warenne took over the manor of Cherchefelle as the king had promised. He chose to build his stronghold on a sandstone mound a little further west. Gradually a new settlement grew up to the south in the shelter of the castle walls, and by 1170 this had come to be known as Reygate. This name could have several meanings, but the most plausible is 'the way of the stream', for the Rie - or Wray - joins with the Lesbourne and turns westwards to provide a water supply for the growing population - convenient particularly, as we shall see, for a priory.

Near their castles, which were symbols of their earthly power, the Warennes established religious houses, symbols of their faith and devotion. These were priories - small monasteries governed by a Prior. At Lewes and Castle Acre they built Cluniac priories but when William de Warenne, the sixth Earl of Surrey, founded his priory at Reigate, he gave it to the new and popular Order of St Augustine, for a community of regular canons. He was following the lead of his parents, who had already presented the church at Reigate to the Augustinian Priory of St Mary Overie at Southwark.

The Augustinian Canons

The Augustinian Order had reached England around 1100 A.D. They followed the rules laid down by Augustine, the Bishop of Hippo in Africa in 395 A.D., (not the Augustine who brought Christianity to Canterbury 200 years later). They came to be known as Black Canons, for they wore a long black cassock, lined with sheepskin in winter, with a white knee-length surplice. Over this was a black cloak, fastened at the neck, with an elbow-length cape and a hood. Unlike monks from other orders, who always shaved, canons wore beards. On their heads they wore rather tall square-cut black caps.

These 'regular canons' had more freedom than monks, and though they observed the rituals, their vows included service to the world outside. Their priory would be a home for a religious community centred around a church; it would provide a hospital, a dispensary, a refuge for the poor and

An Augustinian Canon.

homeless, a school, a guest house for travellers of all classes - pilgrims, merchants and even kings.

Similar priories in London had hospitals which have survived to this day, as St Bartholomew's and St Thomas's, but here in Reigate, the 'hospitium' aspect seems to have been predominant only in the first hundred years.

William de Warenne established the Priory as a separate manor - Manorium Prioratus de Reygate. As Manning and Bray wrote, in their mighty *History of the Antiquities of Surrey*, he gave the canons 'a parcel of the demesnes of this manor, first for their habitation, then for their support'. He chose the best possible location for the Priory, not far from the castle and the main street, on a level site, and close to the water supply, the Wray stream. For the ongoing income, the Warennes endowed the Priory with a number of properties in and around Reigate, such as Littleton Farm and Wonham water mill, with farms at Horley, and with certain revenues from West Humble, Mickleham, Capel and from the manor of Southwick, near Lewes.

Ellis Peters' medieval whodunnits, portraying Brother Cadfael, the herbalist cum detective at Shrewsbury Abbey, give us a vivid picture of earlier monastic life, in the time of King Stephen. The 'Sancte Crucis de Reygate S. Commune Prioratus', the Priory of the Holy Community of the Holy Cross of Reigate, was founded in the colourful and formative period of Richard Coeur de Lion, the Crusades and King John.

People were divided by the language they spoke - English by the peasants, French by the upper classes and Latin by the priests and men of law. But a framework of justice was developing; peasants

were no longer slaves and even the king's tyranny was curbed. Surprisingly, it was King John's supporter, our William de Warenne, who eventually managed to persuade him to sign the Magna Carta in 1215.

The Priory in Reigate

Here at Reigate, William de Warenne, the Priory's Founder, was succeeded in 1240 by his son John, a dramatic and aggressive character who is notorious for flourishing his ancient rusty sword to assert ownership of his lands. It was fiery John who in 1279 won for Reigate the right to have a weekly market and five fair days a year. Amazingly, he lived to the ripe old age - for those days - of 75.

The building of Reigate Priory must have taken many years to complete. The church was of primary importance, but it may have taken several decades to finish it. The simpler living quarters, the dormitory and the refectory would be built first, then the guest house, hospitium and infirmary. The powerful Warenne family had their own experienced builders and craftsmen, but the canons would roll up their sleeves and kilt their tunics to serve by contributing their labour.

We cannot be sure of the outward appearance of the original Priory, but we know it was built of Reigate stone, perhaps supplied by Roger of Reigate, Peter of Merstham or Randolph of Reigate, who were selling large quantities of local stone for Westminster Abbey at that time, at six shillings a hundredweight. We can guess the Priory layout and dimensions, for some of the foundations survive beneath and around the present structure. Parts of the cellar remain, but most of the crypt has been filled in with concrete.

The main entrance was from the west. Park Lane ran south from the old market place, then a track led over the stream to the gatehouse and on to the Great West Door of the Priory Church.

Parts of the walls of the church still remain, forming the present main hall, which is about 70 feet long. The Lady Chapel, beyond the chancel at the east end, is now used as the Headteacher's office. At the west end, hidden in the wall to the north of the main staircase, are the three arches which gave access from the north west porch to the nave, where the townspeople came to hear mass. The position of the Great West Door can be seen in the former Library, now the Museum, behind the 17th century staircase.

Reigate stone in the Priory's East wall, original building materials revealed by renovations in 1988.

A further reminder of the monastic origins appeared in the early 1980s when experts looked for the cause of the crack above the three arches. This work revealed a small room hidden in the thickness of the wall, where we discovered a medieval window frame and traces of simple wall paintings. This room could have been a watching chamber, similar to those at Canterbury Cathedral and the church of St Bartholomew the Great. From this window the people entering the Great West Door, and indeed the whole church, could be surveyed. A medieval security system?

We can shut our eyes and, in imagination, smell the scent of incense pervading the Priory. The church would be dimly lit by a few flickering candles, and burning wicks in the wall cressets. Shafts of light came from high narrow window slits. Pictures of saints and Bible scenes were painted on the walls. In the winter the cold stone floor would have been strewn with dried sweet rushes.

Where the hall narrows for the chancel there must have been a rood screen, and at each end of the church, arched doorways through the south wall would have led to the cloisters, surrounding the square garth. Bones of the canons have been found buried under the grass there, for this was their graveyard. The long building behind the western cloister would have been used for the prior's lodging. Behind the eastern cloister would be the Chapter House and dormitory, and the southern range would have held the refectory, with perhaps a detached kitchen.

What may have been the foundations of that southern range, just north of the sunk garden, still remain three or four feet below ground level. They were revealed in 1993, when electric cables were being laid for flood-lighting. Early local maps show the position of the H-shaped gatehouse, fifty feet or so from the Great West Door.

It is likely that the massive foundations to the north east of the present building, excavated in 1993 when new drains were being laid to take surface water from the Safeways car park, supported the

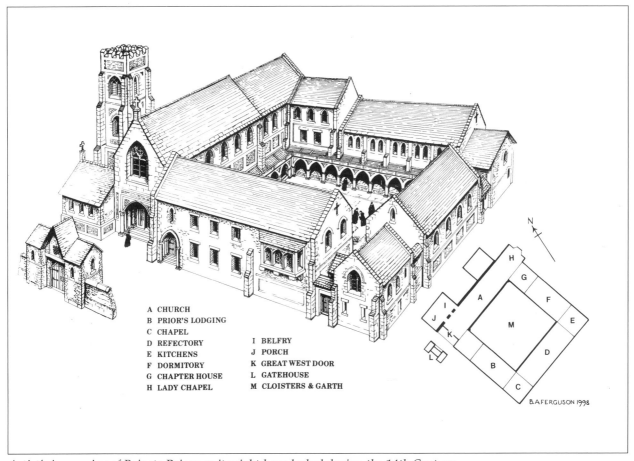

A CHURCH
B PRIOR'S LODGING
C CHAPEL
D REFECTORY
E KITCHENS
F DORMITORY
G CHAPTER HOUSE
H LADY CHAPEL
I BELFRY
J PORCH
K GREAT WEST DOOR
L GATEHOUSE
M CLOISTERS & GARTH

B.A.FERGUSON 1998

Artist's impression of Reigate Priory as it might have looked during the 14th Century.

The seal of Reigate Priory.

guest house or infirmary. These foundations and buttresses are surprisingly substantial - and exciting - for some of the fragments of masonry showed that the building had been 'of a particularly fine Gothic style'.

The Priory was, of course, surrounded by many acres of land. The level area would be cultivated for fruit and vegetables and for basic crops, to feed themselves and their animals. Herbs were grown for cooking and medicines. The little stream, running north of the building, would have been used for irrigation, but we know that a culvert carried water along the east side, presumably for washing purposes and for cleansing the 'necessarium' which housed the very basic lavatories. The main stream ran westwards and, at a suitable distance from the Priory, was diverted to create a system of fish ponds - essential for their food supply.

Gifts to the Priory

Ancient documents, some now preserved in Winchester and Cambridge, show us that over the years, pious local people made gifts of adjoining land:-

In 1317 Jefferey Wallensis and Ann his wife granted 19 acres of meadow and pasture abutting upon Priory land to the west and upon the hill south.

In 1329 William Clarke of Nutfield granted 50 acres, called Brokes.

In 1334 Alan de Warlwyk and Emma his wife granted the Priory a house, a mill, 155 acres of land, nine acres of wood, in Horley and Burstow, as endowment for daily celebration of masses.

In 1391 Alice Skynner granted 'eight acres and a half of meadow called Park Pond Meade, that part of it where the piece of water is, lying adjacent to lands called Seale Hill on the south and bounded by Park Lane on the west'. Presumably before that the pond area was rented.

Life in the Priory

For more than 300 years daily life at the Priory revolved around the framework of services, each preceded by the ringing of the great bell and punctuated by the tinkling of little bells - Matins, Lauds and Prime before daybreak, Tierce, Sext and Nones during the day, then Vespers and Compline in the evening. Prayers and psalms were sung or recited, in Latin.

There would be two complete meals a day, mainly of bread, or porridge made from beans and peas washed down with ale. We know they had a dove house and a warren, so pigeon and rabbit, as well as fish and eggs, must have been served occasionally.

Here at Reigate Priory, for many of the earlier years the chief official was called the Master or Warden. We know that a certain Brother Henry was appointed as Warden in 1253. At this time Reigate Priory was known as the Hospital of the Holy Cross, but later, perhaps as the building was completed and became fully operational, the title of the chief official became 'Prior'. Prior Adam was appointed in 1298. From that time the Bishops' Registers give us the names of all his successors until the Dissolution in 1536. The Prior was usually selected from the Canons of St Mary Overie, but elected and confirmed by the canons of the Reigate community.

Many of the canons had other official duties. The sacristan was in charge of the buildings, banners, robes, the candles and the altar vessels. The Infirmarian cared for the sick and old. The Almoner doled out food and clothing for the poor, the lepers and beggars. The Guest-master looked after visitors and pilgrims. The Cellarer organised supplies of food, drink and fuel. The Chamberlain was responsible for the canons' clothing, bedding, weekly foot washing and baths four or five times a year, head shaving every three weeks, and even blood-letting at regular intervals!

There would be a Precentor responsible for everything to do with music, a Librarian to care for the precious books and to oversee the scriptorium in the cloisters where books were skilfully copied by hand. Some of the books now preserved in the Cranston Library may possibly originate from Reigate Priory. These two - and half a dozen more - are certainly relevant:-

Horae Beatae Mariae Virginis cum Calendario (The Hours of the Blessed Virgin Mary with a calendar) Augustini Epistolae (Letters of Augustine).

Augustinian canons took in local boys and taught them to read and write - so Reigate Priory was a school even then! Some of these boys would become novices and eventually make their vows and join the Order.

The canons were not confined within the Priory walls. They knew and worked with the townspeople and served God by serving the wider community, mingling with the crowds in the market place and taking turns to pray in the chantry chapels, one up at the castle, the chapel of the Holy Cross near the old market place at the west end of the High Street, the chapel of St Thomas À Becket at the east end and the chapel of St Lawrence in what is now Bell Street.

Some of the men living here would have been lay brothers who performed the various necessary jobs, skilled or mundane. These were men not willing or able to make the lifetime vows, binding them to devotion and celibacy.

The day-to-day affairs of the Priory were discussed by the prior and canons each morning when they met in the Chapter House. Sometimes the Bishop would be present, making his routine visitation. The records of these meetings were written up in the Bishop's Registers.

What we find in the Bishop's Registers

These have survived and are preserved in the Diocesan Records Office at Winchester. To turn the soft pages of vellum is an unforgettable experience. The pricked guide lines, the occasional ink blots and alterations, the odd drip of candle wax and the little caricature of one of the brethren, drawn to embellish the first letter on a page - all these bring to life for us the scribes who laboured here centuries ago.

The language they used was, of course, Latin,

Page from Bishop's Register with initial 'K' for 'Kalendis' with caricature enlarged.

using the letter forms, the abbreviations and specialised vocabulary of the time, so it is difficult for us to make a translation.

But we can recognise that on one page there is a list of priors and abbots who assembled for some important occasion - perhaps to elect some diocesan official. There were the abbots of Winchester, Titchfield, Netley, Waverley and Bermondsey, and the priors of Reigate, Tandridge, Newark, Merton and Mottisfont - and a dozen more.

We read that in 1298 in the time of Prior Adam, there were two London merchants, William Sebane and Ralph Hosier, who became generous benefactors, then decided to join the Order themselves. Others whose names are recorded paid a 'carrody' and lived out the rest of their days at the Priory, without taking vows. An early form of sheltered accommodation! The register records gifts of money as well as property.

When Prior Froyle retired in 1309 he was allowed a pension and a chamber in the house. It is obvious that his successor, Prior Walter de Timberden, was not very pleased about that.

It was in 1317 while Timberden was Prior, that John de Warenne abducted Alice de Lacey and

Bishop Waynflete's Register c. 1400.

the 14th century and the Wars of the Roses in the 15th, but their effects percolated through, especially to life in an Augustinian priory, which was not strict and sequestered, but had one foot in the world.

There must have been some times of intense busy-ness. The preparations and the expense for the visitation of a bishop with his large retinue, or of some powerful secular figure, must have taxed all their resources. The infamous John Howard, Duke of Norfolk, stayed here for a few days in September 1483. It is recorded, however, that he paid the Priory Steward 20 pence as a pious offering and paid generously for fuel, light and provisions. Two years later, Howard died at Bosworth Field.

The last of the Priors

The 15th century was a time of great change. Wycliffe had translated the Bible into English, Caxton's press had replaced the monastic scribe and the printed Bible was available for all who could read. The Reformation was on its way.

brought her to Reigate Castle. In reprisal, her husband put Warenne's northern castle of Wakefield to the torch. Though many of the stories of Robin Hood are legendary, some historians believe he was the son of a forester in the service of John de Warenne at Wakefield and that Robin was outlawed for being a follower of Alice's husband, the Earl of Lancaster.

These worldly scandals, including John de Warenne's many other dastardly deeds, are not, of course, recorded in the register - but they do give us glimpses of the historical background.

Later that century, on 14th October 1374, during a vacancy between priors, Bishop Wykeham forbade the sub-prior to allow townspeople to attend services in the Priory church, to the neglect of their parish church - under pain of excommunication. Strong words! Parishioners were accused of going on Sundays and festivals to an early mass at the Priory church, 'and before that was scarcely over, hurrying off to spend their time in drinking booths or in other profane and dishonourable occupations'.

At that time the Priory community could hardly have escaped the ravages of the Black Death, which almost halved the population. Wars must have seemed remote - the Hundred Years War came in

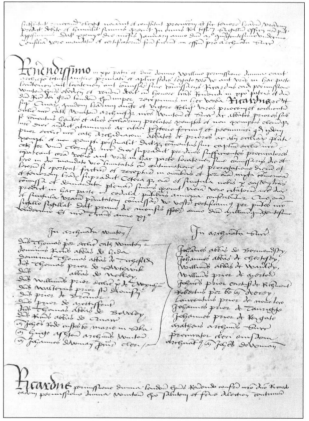

In this page alone, there are many clues to further discovery.

Here at Reigate the last four priors, Robert Mitchell, John Robson, William Major and John Lymden, played a double rôle as both Prior and Vicar of Reigate Parish Church.

John Lymden, our last Prior, is of special interest. We know that he was a canon from St Mary Overie at Southwark, and that he was elected Prior of Reigate on 28th November 1530. In 1975 we tracked down an ancient portrait, painted in oils on wood, which is said to portray him. It had been put on record, and even photographed, by the National Portrait Gallery in the 1850s. Later it was acquired by Sir George Bellew, Keeper of the Rolls, who generously offered it to the Priory Museum for a token sum, so now the picture is back home, in John Lymden's Priory. The gold shells on the Tudor cap are badges showing that Lymden had made numerous pilgrimages to Santiago de Compostella. The palm leaf is a symbol that he had visited the Holy Land. The seventeen rings on his fingers would be gifts from priors who had given him hospitality on his journeyings.

When the Priory was dissolved on 26th July 1536 Lymden received an annual pension of £10 for life - which was still being paid in 1553. It is likely that he married and had a family, for the name continued to appear in local records. His name is perpetuated in Reigate to this day, but now as a street name not far from his Priory.

Four canons stayed with Lymden to the end: Robert Kanam was then transferred to St Bartholomew's and Thomas Kendall to St Mary Overie. Clerical appointments were found for Richard Dowtie and Robert Aires.

The candles were snuffed out. Valuables were transferred to the royal coffers. Sacred books and manuscripts may have been taken over to the parish church. Commissioners arrived to suppress the house on the feast of St Anne - 26th July - in 1536. They assessed its value at £68. Lord Edmund Howard, a son of Lord Thomas Howard, the Earl of Surrey, was appointed as steward, to manage the Priory properties and to collect all the rents and tithes. The Priory buildings and the grounds were let to a Mr John Martin.

In 1539 Edmund died, but the Howard star was rising. In 1541, his daughter Catherine became Queen of England, and the Priory was granted to Edmund's older half-brother, William Howard.

After 300 years as a holy place of worship and of service to the community, of sombrely clad Black Canons living by the rule of St Augustine, of incense and candles, of plainsong and bells, Reigate Priory became a vibrant, warm and colourful home to an important Tudor family, with impressive royal connections.

Four centuries on – the Earl and Countess of Effingham
view the memorial to the Earl's ancestor, Charles Howard, Lord High Admiral.

THREE HOWARDS AND THEIR HOME

'Another Historic Chapter' - this was the *Surrey Mirror*'s headline for a page of photographs recording an important occasion for Reigate and for the Priory. On a cold bright Monday, 5th December 1988, Mowbray Howard, Earl of Effingham, stood with his charming Countess on the chancel steps of Reigate St Mary's Parish Church. This was truly a historic occasion. They are shown looking up intently at the gleaming brass memorial which commemorates the achievements of the Earl's illustrious ancestor, Charles, Lord Howard of Effingham, Earl of Nottingham, Queen Elizabeth's Lord High Admiral, who in 1588 defeated 'the Spaniards' Invincible Navy'.

Beneath their feet, in the family vault, piled one upon the other, lay numerous Howards - the great Admiral himself, his parents William and Margaret, his brother William and his son Charles, along with various nephews and nieces. Who were these Howards?

The blue and gold chequers in the third quarter of the Howard shield give us a clue. In the 14th century, Edmund, Earl of Arundel, married Alice de Warenne, who inherited the estates of John, Earl of Warenne and Surrey. Five generations later, through various marriages, we find that their descendants are the Howards, Earls of Surrey and Dukes of Norfolk.

William Howard

By the time of Henry VIII these Howards had great power and influence at court. Royal favour fell especially upon William, born in 1509, the year of the King's accession, and though William was 18 years younger than the King, they became personal friends. They hunted and played tennis together - William was given his own suite of apartments at Hampton Court Palace. The King chose Lord William to accompany him to Calais for the meeting with the French King, a magnificent assembly known as 'The Field of the Cloth of Gold'. Later, William acted as Earl Marshal at the coronation of his own niece, Anne Boleyn.

He was entrusted on various occasions with difficult negotiations with James V of Scotland. In December 1539 it was William again who was

Lord William, 1st Baron Howard of Effingham.

chosen for the delicate task of meeting Anne of Cleves, selected unseen to be Henry's fourth bride. His brief was to welcome her in Calais, the last English possession across the channel, as she first put her foot on English soil, then to escort her by ship to England to meet her royal bridegroom. While they were detained for two weeks 'for want of a prosperous wind' Anne came to like and trust William and she asked him to teach her to play cent, the King's favourite card game. But the King could not bear the prospect of married life with this 'Flemish mare', and the marriage was short-lived. Anne quietly and tactfully retired from public life. William Howard and Anne of Cleves remained good friends until her death in 1557, when William was an executor and took a leading part in her funeral.

Fortunately, the King liked William Howard and expressed his trust by making him a Knight of the Garter and appointing him to be Lord High Admiral. A peak in the Howard family fortunes came in 1540, when Henry chose another of William's nieces, Catherine Howard, to be his fifth bride - Queen of England.

At this time of joy, the King was generous with gifts to his friends. He had acquired a considerable amount of property as a result of closing scores of the smaller monasteries, and some of these he gave to his supporters.

To William Howard he first gave the Manor and Priory of Tottenham, but when he realised that the area could usefully extend his hunting grounds, he changed his mind.

So instead, on 8th June 1541, he granted 'the Manor and Priory of Reigate, from the King to Lord William Howard. The said King, by letters patent, grants to William Lord Howard and Margaret his wife and the heirs of their bodies, in exchange for the Rectory Manor of Tottenham in Middlesex, the House and Site of the late dissolved Priory of Reigate.' This was carved out of the manor of Reigate to create a separate manor.

The Howards owned Reigate Priory for the next 140 years. Lord William would have used his house at Lambeth for his official duties, but he came to regard Reigate Priory as his family home. To convert the old monastic building into a Tudor mansion only adaptation and modernisation were needed.

But before the changes could possibly have been completed, Lord William lost everything - or so it seemed. When the King learned that his captivating queen, Catherine Howard, might have been unfaithful, his fury fell upon her relations. Lord William and his wife Margaret were imprisoned in the Tower 'for ever' and deprived

This engraving from Memoirs of the Earls of Warenne and Surrey is an artist's impression of the Priory in 1577, after William Howard's adaptation. Some details are known to be inaccurate.

The New Market House Reigate, adapted from the medieval chantry chapel of St Thomas à Becket, looking west.

of their properties. Sir John Gorstwick and John Skinner took an inventory of all their belongings and Bishop Cranmer and Lady Oxford became responsible for the young Howard children. Fortunately, after some months, the King relented, Lord William and his wife were released and their properties restored to them.

Their first view of Reigate, when they returned some time in 1543, must have filled them with joy. Like the Black Canons three centuries earlier, they would have approached the little town from Nettley (now Nutley) Lane, ridden across the old market place by the Red Cross Inn, then, I like to think, on this unusual occasion, taken the longer route east along the High Street, between the overhanging, tightly packed houses, inns and workshops. We can picture the townspeople leaning out of their windows or running alongside, waving and shouting their greetings with delight. Could it perhaps have been a market day when, added to the population of just a few hundreds, there were farmers, traders, countrywomen with their baskets of produce, and entertainers performing in the new market place around the disused chantry chapel of Thomas à Becket?

Here they would turn right, and the horses would slow as they splashed through the sandy stream which made its way across Bell Lane. Then, passing the shrine of Our Lady of Ouldsworth, set in the old Priory wall, they could have entered their home by an eastern gate, thrown open wide to welcome them safely back again.

The Priory becomes a home

Parts of the ancient buildings had to be demolished, but some evidence remains - fortunately, mechanical diggers were not available at that time to devastate the site. In 1993, trenches for new drains were being dug beside the Priory Car Park in Bell Street, when massive sections of mortared stonework were uncovered. The Surrey Archaeological Unit was given only two weeks for an exploratory 'dig'. This revealed ancient foundations of walls over a metre thick, constructed from roughly hewn Reigate stone blocks, bonded with lime mortar. Pottery sherds from the building suggest it was constructed in the 13th century, while sherds from the rubble

resulting from its demolition were of 16th century date. As we have already seen, the building, beside an eastern entrance to the Priory grounds, may have been the Guest House or Infirmary - no longer required by the new Howard owners.

The buildings on the south side of the cloister garth were also demolished. We know that these foundations remain, parallel to the hedge along the north side of the sunken garden. They were most recently uncovered in 1993, when cables for floodlighting were being laid.

Next, an extra floor was constructed in the nave of the old church, creating a great hall at ground level, with bedrooms above. Staircases to these were probably constructed in the north west and north east wings, where staircases still exist today.

Stone mullioned and transom window, still in its original position in an upstairs wall.

A chimney or a window? The mysterious corbels, originally on the exterior north wall of the Priory showing that an extra floor was installed by the Howards.

Stone mullioned windows were set into the outer walls to admit light and, on the south front, to open up views of the park. One of these stone frames has remained for over 400 years, in perfect condition, encased in an upstairs wall at the back.

A great fireplace was built into the north wall of the former church, with the Howard arms carved in the pointed arch, and a lion rampant, Lord William's personal badge, carved at each corner. On the outside, a huge chimney stack was constructed with three elegant Tudor brick chimneys on top.

At first floor level we have an intriguing mystery, for there are four large stone corbels jutting out from the chancel wall. Could these have supported a chimney, or perhaps, an oriel window, facing north across the courtyard, towards the fashionable Tudor Tennis House, newly built of brick? Unfortunately this building was destroyed by fire in 1575, thirty years later, but the present structure on that site incorporates some of the original Reigate stone and sixteenth-century bricks. Real, or royal, tennis was a most popular sport with King Henry and his courtiers, so the Tennis House here must have been the centre of many colourful and lively sporting events.

The old Lady Chapel at the church's east end was retained and used by the Howards and later owners as their family chapel. The Reigate stone structure was revealed in the 1980s when the plaster facing was repaired.

The great gatehouse stayed too, perhaps used now as an impressive entrance from the west.

Henry VIII died in 1547, but William lived for another 26 years, loyal to three more monarchs. Edward VI granted to him the manors of Effingham and Great Bookham; then in 1554, as a reward for quelling the Wyatt Rebellion, Queen Mary I conferred upon him the title of Baron Howard of Effingham.

When he died in 1573, he left instructions for the construction of a family vault beneath the South Chancel of the Parish Church, so there he lies, with his wife Margaret and many of his

Charles, Lord Howard of Effingham, First Earl of Nottingham.

descendants, and with subsequent owners of Reigate Priory.

It was Lord William who established the Howards as a family constantly loyal to their sovereign, always capable, adaptable, tactful and dignified. Yet it was his son Charles who inherited and displayed these qualities with greatest effect.

Charles Howard – the Priory's most famous owner

Charles was born in 1536, probably in Lambeth. From the age of five he spent much of his childhood at Reigate Priory. He grew up to become one of the most highly regarded personalities of the Elizabethan age. His life and his exploits, especially his leading rôle in the defeat of the Spanish Armada in 1588, are so well documented that there seems little more to discover.

But our hunt for Priory clues and connections led to some remarkable experiences.

When Miles Howard, 17th Duke of Norfolk, visited the Priory in April 1988, to open our Armada exhibition, he suggested we should invite his cousin Mowbray Howard, the Earl of Effingham. This led to the visit of the Earl and Countess of Effingham in the following November.

The Effinghams so enjoyed their visit that they asked to be allowed to express their thanks by inviting us to tea at the Palace of Westminster to see the House of Lords where the Armada tapestries once hung. As a surprise, they arranged for us to see the Pine engravings of the original designs, now held by the House of Lords Library, and to present us with a slide and a print for our museum collection.

As a bonus, the Earl drew from his pocket, and placed in my hand for a few minutes, the exquisite Hilliard miniature of his ancestor. This gave me my closest encounter with the great Admiral.

But, for the record, we must return to historical facts.

In his teens, the young Charles Howard was educated for a time by John Foxe, author of the *Book of Martyrs*. (It was the Protestant John Foxe who was responsible for the removal of the shrine of Our Lady of Ouldsworth.) Sometimes at the Priory and sometimes at Reigate Castle, Charles' companions were his orphaned cousins, the

Catherine Carey, Countess of Nottingham.

family of Henry Howard, Earl of Surrey, who had been beheaded in 1547. The children would have studied French, Latin, Law, Penmanship and, no doubt, Divinity.

Charles then served as a page to his cousin Thomas, later Fourth Duke of Norfolk. Fishing, hunting, training in 'chivalric exercise at arms' - all these were 'de rigueur'. At 18 he was sent to France to the household of the Vidame de Chartres - but soon he returned home. Apparently, he had not been treated as a young nobleman should be treated! From that time he often went to sea with his father and built up a wealth of useful experience.

Although he was first cousin to Anne Boleyn, the mother of Queen Elizabeth, he was three years younger than Elizabeth herself. He was a handsome young man with 'an eminently fine person and countenance, a sweet frank temper and a deportment at once elegant and dignified'. He was even mentioned as a possible candidate for the Queen's hand - but instead, he married the Queen's favourite Maid of Honour, Catherine

Carey. In 1572 Catherine became First Lady of the Chamber, supervising the Queen's enormous and expensive wardrobe and her jewels. She was the Queen's closest friend, and was a wife of 'irreproachable conduct'.

But Charles became Chamberlain of the Royal Household. This gave him a seat on the Privy Council, a salary of £133 6s 8d, a table at Court, a livery and powers of patronage. As Chamberlain, he directed:-

    The Wardrobe, The Jewel House,
    The Kitchen, bakery and spicery,
    The Banqueting Hall and Lodgings in the
      Palace,
    Royal Chaplains, Chapel and Vestry,
    Surgeons and Apothecaries,
    Painters and Astronomers,
    Mole-takers and Masters of Hounds,
    Royal Parks and Deer Herds,
    The Queen's Ordnance,
    The Mint,
    The Reception of foreign ambassadors at
      Court, etc. etc.

More honours and responsibilities followed. He became a Companion of the Order of the Garter in 1575. He served as M.P. for Surrey and Lord Lieutenant for Surrey and Sussex. In 1587 he was chosen to be one of the commissioners who tried Mary Queen of Scots.

The Queen put great trust in him, and he was made responsible for her personal security. She allotted to him a suite of rooms at Nonsuch Palace, and this arrangement continued even into the following reign.

The Lord High Admiral

In 1585, when the threat from Spain had become serious, Queen Elizabeth appointed Charles Howard to be her Lord High Admiral - 'Lieutenant General and Commander in Chief of the Navy and Army prepared to the seas against Spain'. Such great seamen as Frobisher, Hawkins and Drake had far more skill and experience, but Lord Charles Howard of Effingham had the dignity of noble birth, giving him unquestionable

The Ark Royal – note the Howard standard.

authority. He had excellent qualities of leadership. He had foresight and patience, he was firm and fair, he could handle difficult personalities, even the Queen. He could inspire confidence and he was generous with praise and encouragement.

When the Queen became anxious about the mounting costs of keeping the army and navy waiting for the Spanish fleet to appear, she ordered her lieutenants to send their armies home, and her Lord Admiral to disband the fleet. But Charles Howard used 'freedom to disobey' and even offered to retain all the ships in service at his own expense. So on July 19th 1588, when the Armada appeared, his fleet was ready.

There was a chain of beacons to signal the invasion, but we were astonished to discover from John Janaway's book on *Surrey* that the armada beacons were never fired. According to Maldon's *History of Surrey*, published in 1900, written orders made it clear that the beacons were to be lighted only if the enemy landed - and as they never did, they never were - except twice earlier, once by vandals and once by mistake, when men were trying to smoke out a badger. The combination of the Lord High Admiral's tactics, his superior ships and the weather, forced the Spanish fleet to sail through the stormy North Sea and round the rocky coasts of Scotland and Ireland, where many of them were wrecked.

Yet, four hundred years later, in July 1988, a beacon and bonfire blazed in the park at Reigate Priory and thousands of local people delighted in a stupendous display of fireworks, celebrating the successes of Reigate's Lord High Admiral. Reigate still commemorates Charles Howard's famous flagship by adopting the modern *Ark Royal* - an aircraft carrier! The Reigate Unit of the Sea Cadet Corps is also called *Ark Royal*.

Wisely, Charles Howard kept his *Ark Royal* mobilised, for the Spaniards prepared to try again. In 1596, with Raleigh and Essex he attacked Cadiz. At last Charles Howard was rewarded with a title which had been held by his ancestors, the Mowbrays. He became Earl of Nottingham.

Essex resented the honours heaped upon the Lord High Admiral and this discontent led to his rebellion in 1601. This was suppressed by Charles Howard, who also took a leading part in his trial. Essex was imprisoned in the Tower and condemned to death.

There is a story that earlier, when Essex was in favour with the Queen, she had given him a ring and told him that if ever he should be in danger, he had only to send it to her and she would save him. He sent it now, but by mistake, the page delivered it to Catherine Howard, Countess of Nottingham, instead of her sister, Lady Scrope, who was in attendance on the Queen at that time. Catherine deliberately withheld the ring and Essex was beheaded. On her deathbed the Countess confessed to the Queen what had happened, but Elizabeth answered 'God may forgive you, but I never can'. It was said that this news hastened the death of the Queen herself. This story is now convincingly discredited, so Catherine's reputation remains 'irreproachable'.

Charles Howard showed great compassion for his disabled and injured sailors, and when the Queen failed to authorise funds to support them, he bore the expense himself. Later, with Drake and Hawkins, he founded the Chatham Chest, a fund eventually used to create the Chelsea Hospital.

In Reigate on the southern edge of his Priory estate, Setby's farm was held by the Ganders family, bondsmen for generations. He released them to be free men and soon they rose to be leading local citizens. Clearly, Charles Howard respected the lives of ordinary people, whether sailors or farm-workers.

'Seven standing houses'

Reigate Priory was not Charles Howard's only home. He is said to have owned 'seven standing houses'.

Skynners Place at Deptford Green near Greenwich was close to the naval docks and came to be regarded as the official residence of the Lord High Admiral.

Arundel House on the Strand was used mainly for magnificent entertainments and sumptuous repasts, often for the Queen and her court. In this house Charles Howard hung the ten great tapestries he had commissioned, showing the destruction of the Spanish Armada. Enriched with gold and silver threads, these must have been dazzling and impressive. The Admiral did not present these to the Queen, as had been expected, but after his death they were displayed in the House of Lords, to be burned to cinders in 1834. Curiously, one escaped, for it had been taken down to make way for a new door. Where it is

John Pine's engraving of Charles Howard's Armada Tapestry, showing the English pursuing the Spanish fleet east of Plymouth.

now, no one knows. Fortunately, Pine's engravings of all the tapestries remain in the House of Lords Library.

Effingham Manor had been granted to Charles' father in 1560, when the title 'Howard of Effingham' was conferred. Charles often lent this house to relations and did not use it himself. It still stands, now called 'Browns'.

Bletchingley was one of the manors given by Henry VIII to his divorced wife Anne of Cleves. Lord William Howard bought it in 1560. It was at Bletchingley church that Charles was married to Catherine Carey on 25th July 1563 and in 1579 their son William was baptised there. Queen Elizabeth visited the Howards at Bletchingley on 17th November 1578. The church accounts record the charge of '6d. on ringing for the Queen'. Later, Charles gave this property to young William as a wedding present. Bletchingley Place was, at that time, almost a palace, but now only the gatehouse remains, converted for modern use and known as Place Farm.

Chelsea Manor House was another house which the Howards often used. It was a gift from the Queen, who often came there to visit her close

friend, Charles Howard's wife.

Reigate Priory was most used as the Howard family home. Did Queen Elizabeth come here to admire the famous herd of deer or the unusual water spaniels which Charles Howard bred here? She may have made a private visit, just as her father may have come here to play in the Tennis House. We do not know, but we do know that the Earl and Countess entertained lavishly.

In the 1580s and '90s Charles Howard had his own theatrical company 'The Lord Admiral's Company of Players'. Though they performed mainly in London - often at Lord Howard's own theatre the Fortune, we know they travelled to such places as Nottingham, Bath, Coventry and Dover. So it is more than likely that the company, including such famous actors as the great Edward Alleyn, entertained Charles Howard's guests at the Priory.

We learn from Dr Hooper's *History of Reigate* that the Admiral maintained a large household at the Priory. His retainers included a clerk of the kitchen, brewer, butler, several cooks, a park keeper, warrener, falconer, horse keeper, mason and rent-gatherer. A terrible outbreak of plague occurred in Reigate in 1603, and several of the Lord Howard's servants were amongst the dead.

Haling House in Croydon was granted by the Queen to Charles Howard in 1592. It was surrounded by an extensive park, noted for its fine trees. Surprisingly, when he was 67 years old, Charles Howard married the 19-year-old Lady Margaret Stewart and their son Charles was born at Haling House. Now, four centuries later, Nottingham Road in Croydon bounds the north edge of Haling Park, where Whitgift School was built in the 1930s.

Charles Howard, Earl of Nottingham

Odd clues turn up sometimes. In 1979 there was an archaeological dig just north of the Priory. Analysis of the debris revealed 17 tomato seeds, the earliest to be recorded in England. Could William or Charles Howard have acquired tomatoes on his travels to Europe (where edible tomatoes were developed from a South American plant) and served these 'apples of love' as a delicacy or a talking point at a Priory banquet 400 years ago? When Miles Howard, the present Duke of Norfolk, came to our Priory Banquet on October 11th 1985, perhaps we should have included tomatoes on the menu! On the other hand, the tomatoes may have had no connection with the Priory.

When Queen Elizabeth was dying it was to her friend and kinsman Charles Howard, Earl of Nottingham, that she made clear her wish that James, King of Scots, should reign after her. The Queen's funeral at Westminster Abbey took place very soon after Lady Nottingham's burial at Chelsea.

Life was never quite the same for Charles Howard. His new marriage and his second family naturally caused gossip. Lady Margaret was cousin to the new King, but Charles Howard and James I never became close friends.

King James wanted peace with Spain, but the illustrious Lord High Admiral was held in such high regard that he was allowed to retain his high office. There is an interesting picture of the Somerset House Peace Conference in 1604, where we see Charles Howard, Earl of Nottingham, resplendent in a suit of white satin, everyone else in sombre black. The next year the King sent him to Spain, with a budget of £15,000, to ratify the treaty. His splendid retinue was all in apparel of

black velvet and gold, and his magnificent fleet of 200 coaches were in fact too many for the narrow, rocky Spanish roads, but the Lord High Admiral was always impressive and spectacular. He served later on the jury at the trial of Guy Fawkes, but gradually his influence and his income decreased. He retired in 1619 at the age of 83. Although he died at Haling House, on 14th December 1624, aged 88 years, his body was buried, not with the great in Westminster Abbey, but as he wished, in the family vault at Reigate Parish Church.

At Reigate Priory, Charles Howard is remembered with great pride. This most eminent owner of the Priory was brought to life in 1988 in the Priory Museum's Commemorative Exhibition. He was brilliantly portrayed as Lord High Admiral on the deck of the *Ark Royal*. It was even possible to show the actual prayer book used by Charles and his father William, for this is preserved in the Cranston Library at Reigate Parish Church and was kindly lent by the Trustees. We were astounded to find that a local collector owned an important 400 year old document, signed and sealed by Elizabeth I, commissioning Charles Howard as her Lord High Admiral, and this he kindly lent for display.

Charles' widow, Margaret Stewart, was soon remarried, this time to her former page, William Lord Monson. After their wedding, held privately in the chapel at Reigate Priory, Margaret proudly rode through the town, introducing him to all their neighbours. William was a nephew of Admiral Monson of Kinnersley, only three miles away. It was Monson who felled and sold the timber from the greensand ridge in the Priory park, now a favourite walk and viewpoint. After Margaret's death he clung tenaciously to her property, though, by the will of Charles Howard, the Priory had been left to his grand-daughter Elizabeth, only child of his eldest son William. Lord Monson even mounted cannon outside the Priory in an attempt to frighten her away. Cannon balls and shot have been found in the Priory grounds, so, (who knows?) they could have been fired at that time.

Elizabeth Howard, Countess of Peterborough

Elizabeth Howard had spent much of her childhood at Reigate Priory. She was only twelve when her father died and 21 at the death of her

John Evelyn, the diarist.

James Ussher, Archbishop of Armagh.

grandfather the Lord High Admiral. Elizabeth was both wealthy and beautiful. She had family connections with England's most powerful families and she was often at Court. Her delightful portrait by Van Dyck can be seen at Wilton House, but copies were greatly prized and are on display in many great houses, including Woburn.

In 1621 when she was 18, she married John Mordaunt, who became Earl of Peterborough. John had been brought up with the royal princes but, surprisingly, fought as a Roundhead for the Commonwealth side in the Civil War. Elizabeth supported him enthusiastically. But their two sons Henry and John joined the opposing Royalist side. Reigate Castle bustled with life again, and it was occupied in turn by Royalists and Parliamentarians. Some shots were fired. Family harmony was shattered and the Howard fortunes dwindled as Elizabeth tried to support both her husband and her two sons.

Bletchingley Place could no longer be maintained and was dismantled around 1650.

Fortunately Elizabeth, Countess of Peterborough, rescued the most important feature, a magnificent Tudor overmantel, and refixed it at Reigate Priory, around the Howard stone fireplace. John Evelyn, a close friend of the Howards and Mordaunts, visited the Priory on August 21st 1655 and recorded in his famous *Diary* that it was 'an ancient monastery well in repair, but the park much defaced; the house is nobly furnished'. Elizabeth had shown to him, 'the chimneypiece in the great chamber - carved in wood'. Its origins are shrouded in mystery, but it is thought to have been commissioned by Henry VIII from the artist Holbein. Experts agree that it must have come originally from one of Henry VIII's palaces, Nonsuch or Bridewell. Today, this architectural treasure, still in place at the Priory, attracts admirers from all over the world.

On that day in 1655, John Evelyn especially enjoyed seeing another friend and guest of the Countess, James Ussher. This great Irish Archbishop was deeply respected for his scholarship, his tolerance and sincerity.

James Ussher is remembered for calculating the dates that are in some editions of the Authorised Version of the Bible, especially for fixing the date of the Creation precisely as 4004 B.C.

By now he was poor, ageing, sick and almost blind, but the Countess cared for him at Reigate Priory until he died from pleurisy on 20th March 1656. His chaplain described how 'his eyesight was extremely decayed by his constant studying so that he could scarce see to write, but at a window, and that in sunshine which he constantly followed on clear days one window to another'.

Simply described scenes like this enrich our present understanding of the Priory, for they help us to appreciate the varied and remarkable personalities who have built up its special atmosphere.

As Elizabeth, Countess of Peterborough, grew older, her son John lived at the Priory with his wife and family. Eventually it came to Mary, the daughter of Elizabeth's elder son Henry. Both Bletchingley Place and Reigate Priory had to be sold to meet the family's debts. The eventful and colourful Howard ownership, which had lasted for 140 years, came to an end.

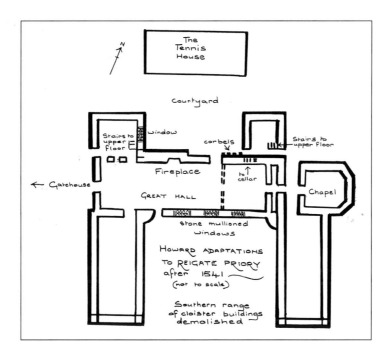

The Parsons' Brewhouse
Just east of the Tower of London. Sir John Parsons boards the Mayoral barge,
September 29th 1703.

TWO LORD MAYORS OF LONDON – AND A BREWERY

*A*brewery, business acumen and black 'beire' were the background to the success of the next two owners of Reigate Priory, John Parsons and his son Humphrey. They were members of the newly emerging class of power, wealthy merchants and business men.

John Parsons was born in 1643, and named John after his father. He lived through the reigns of six sovereigns of England, from Charles I to George I. During his lifetime he saw drastic changes in life, not only in costume and customs, but also in civil and Parliamentary life. In the days of his boyhood and youth, England passed through the upheaval of Civil War and the Commonwealth. At the Restoration in 1660 when young John was 17 he may have taken part in the celebrations to welcome Charles II to the throne.

Around this time John's father bought a brewhouse on the river front, just east of the Tower of London. He named it the Red Lion Brewhouse. Their beer was an entirely different product from ordinary beer, with a higher alcoholic content. It was a stout made from fermented malt, with very little, if any, hops, and it possessed a separate legal definition in the Customs and Excise Acts. It received a tribute from Oliver Goldsmith, who called it 'Parsons' Black Champagne'.

The brewery survived until 1938 and the records are now held by the Bass Museum at Burton-on-Trent. They describe a visit to the brewery in so much detail that one can almost smell the malt, hear the din from the hammering of at least 40 coopers and feel the sharp changes of temperature required for the different processes. I suspect that the secret ingredient was the superb water from the great well, five feet in diameter, sunk a hundred feet through the clay,

sand and chalk. The Thames water was used only for cooling purposes.

On the trail of John Parsons

One cold bright February day, my husband and I set off on our 'Alderman Sir John Parsons Discovery Trail'.

The Red Lion Brewhouse stood near that area which became St Katherine's Dock. Our first discovery, after passing the impressive new Tower Hotel and walking a few steps along St Katherine's Way, was a little stairway between the new buildings fronting the river, 'Alderman Stairs'.

We knew from the 18th Century maps of this area that they were originally known as Alderman **Parsons'** Stairs, and that they led down from the wharf in front of the Red Lion Brewery. As we looked up-river, the camera saw the very new riverside development, the 'new' Tower Bridge, only 100 years old. Yet the Tower itself is still there for us to see, as John Parsons did 300 years ago. We looked up-river with new eyes. **We** saw the rippling waters of the River Thames right up to the old London Bridge with its houses and shops; **we** saw little wherries and shallops, Company barges and cargo boats, perhaps one sailing low in the water laden with casks of the famous 'black champagne'. As we walked back we hardly noticed the modern block of flats on the Red Lion Brewery site; we saw the bustling brewery and smelt the beer and malt. The mounted policeman clopping by on the cobbles was changed in our imagination to a heavy brewer's dray pulled by strong horses with jangling harness.

We looked around for signs of the Hermitage, the large house in which the Parsons family lived, next to the brewery. We found quite near Alderman

Stairs a fairly modern gateway with the name 'Hermitage Garden Centre', though the site was derelict. Nearby there is a twisty backstreet named Hermitage Wall.

Our Parsons discovery trail next took us to the Royal Exchange to look for Exchange Alley where the Parsons had a superior ale-house, 'The Swan', the Hilton of that time. With delight we found the alley, now Change Alley - but no Swan, for that was burned down in 1748.

John Parsons comes to Reigate

As a young man John must have seen the effects of the terrible plague and the great fire of London. Apparently the Parsons family and fortunes were unscathed. In the next year, 1667, when he was 24 years old, John married Elizabeth Beane, a daughter of Humphrey Beane of Epsom - who was a cordwainer (shoe-maker) and an Alderman of the City of London.

John was fond of horses and his father-in-law allowed him to build coach houses and stables on his land there. John later bought this land from his mother-in-law for £230.

By 1677 he was in full charge of the highly successful Red Lion Brewery. Brewers were doing well, for beer was the national beverage - and no wonder, for water supplies were appallingly unhygienic. Tea, coffee and chocolate had been introduced, but beer was still part of the staple diet.

John Parsons became Master of the Brewers' Company, a Freeman of the City of London, and in 1677 he was appointed as one of the Victuallers of the Navy.

In due course John and Elizabeth produced a large family of eleven surviving children. First of all came three sons, John (of course!), then Henry, then Humphrey, of whom we shall hear much more later.

At this time many of the wealthier city merchants were buying estates outside London, but within commuting distance. London was an unhealthy place to live in, for disease, over-crowding, and fogs caused by the increasing use of coal, were spoiling the quality of life.

It was in 1681 that John Parsons bought Reigate Priory. When he bought the manor and lands, the building was already nearly 500 years old, as John Evelyn had described it, after his visit on 21st August 1655, 'An ancient monastery, well in repair'.

John Parsons was buying an impressive property with its own manorial rights, a mansion set in a beautiful park, a healthy home for his growing family.

Their family was indeed increasing, and the three boys were followed by eight daughters, Catherine, Mary, Ann, Marianna, Julianna, Elizabeth, Susannah and Jane. Elizabeth Parsons must have been delighted to bring her little children to live in this beautiful house with its extensive park and bluebell-carpeted woods, its herd of deer, and the herons and other wildfowl by the ponds.

Some of John and Elizabeth Parsons' eight daughters must have been born at the Priory and we know that some were christened and married here in Reigate at the Parish Church. Marianna, for instance, was christened there on August 19th 1690, and Catherine was married there on December 2nd 1694.

Could there have been another reason for the purchase? Not only was John Parsons taking an active part in civic life, but he was getting involved in a new activity - party politics. Did he see Reigate, not only as a pleasant little town to live in, but also as a town to represent in Parliament? In fact, this is how it worked out. He represented Reigate for more than thirty years, almost continuously from 1685 until his death in 1717.

But there were still more reasons for buying Reigate Priory. John Parsons was an ambitious man and saw the value of using his country house for entertaining his friends and business associates.

He decided to embark upon a programme of modernising and embellishing the building.

The Grand Entrance and the Eagle Gates

Owing to his business and official engagements in London, he frequently had to travel between Reigate and the City. Defoe wrote 'Reigate had not one good road, and Alderman Parsons had six of the strongest horses that could be purchased to draw his coach up Reigate Hill'. To meet the needs of himself and his guests, John Parsons provided extra coach houses and stabling, and also an impressive new entrance from Bell Street, on the eastern edge of the estate.

The gateway had handsome pillars surmounted by eagles. They were flanked by screens of fine wrought iron. These were much in fashion, and we can still see splendid examples at Hampton Court. Tijou was the master, but experts tell us that our Priory gateway is more likely to be the work of Thomas Robinson, Tijou's talented assistant. Experts differ in their dating of the ironwork, but

The Eagle Gates in Bell Street c.1710 to 1893. The pointed doorway to the lodge can still be seen.

there is no doubt that John Parsons created the new entrance. A sweeping driveway through the park led to a new main door, with porch and pillars, on the south front.

The Priory gateway can still be seen, with the eagles and the screens, but not in their original position. Lady Henry Somerset moved them to the courtyard 200 years later, in order, we are told, to protect her visitors from the evil influences of the public houses in Bell Street. A belated rebuff for the wealthy brewer!

But the Eagle Gateway was not the only one. There was another splendid wrought iron gateway placed to the north west, near the original monastic entrance in Park Lane - in a slightly different position east of the lodge to enable the lodge-keeper (in the lodge which is still there) to benefit from

The design of the Park Lane gateway.

living in the Old Borough, which terminates there. Incidentally this arrangement brought John Parsons one extra vote! We must remember that the Priory was not part of the Old Borough; it was a separate manor, which lay in what was called 'the Foreign'. The gates were lost some time ago - but that is not the end of the story: they re-appear later in this book!

The Great Hall

John Parsons then turned his attention to the building itself. The ancient monastic bell was recast in 1683 and rehung. The Great Hall had its wonderful fireplace, but almost certainly there were draughts from the Great West Door and from the three open arches to the Priory's old north porch. So these were all bricked up, and now that end of the Great Hall was ready for the construction of a beautiful staircase. A new graceful design was used, with gentle steps, eight feet wide and with two generous landings at the turns. Each stair was edged subtly with a chevron pattern, to echo the chevron on the Parsons coat of arms. Varied designs in marquetry decorated the side-pieces of the steps, and the balusters were turned in different 'barley-sugar' twists. The banister rail too had the chevron pattern running centrally.

Next came the walls and the ceiling - and here John Parsons used his wealth and his influence to excellent effect. Some experts disagree, but the keeper of prints and pictures at the Victoria and Albert Museum asserted that the magnificent murals are by Antonio Verrio, the great Italian artist who worked at Hampton Court, at Chatsworth and, most impressively, at Burghley.

We learn a lot from the Burghley records and accounts. Apparently Verrio painted suspended in a cradle called a 'craike' or on a 'fleake' - a scaffolding tower. He charged about £100 for painting a large room, but blued every penny as soon as he had it.

Walpole described Verrio's paintings as displaying 'heathen gods, goddesses, Christian virtues and allegorical gentlefolks'. Celia Fiennes, the seventeenth-century traveller and diarist, was rather shocked - 'they were all without garments, or very little … especially in My Lord's Apartment'!

Daniel Defoe commented on Verrio's twelve

Sir John Parsons' handsome staircase.

years at Burghley: 'The character this gentleman left behind him at this town, is, that he deserv'd it all for his paintings; but for nothing else; his scandalous life, and his unpaid debts, it seems, causing him to be but very meanly spoken of in the town of Stamford.' We wonder what reputation he left behind in Reigate and which of the alehouses he frequented!

At Reigate Priory we too have gods and goddesses, scantily clothed, floating above us on the ceiling of the staircase, assembled for the marriage of Juno and Jupiter. On the south wall, Pluto is abducting Proserpine, and on the north wall, Man is having great difficulty in choosing between Wisdom and Folly. Below the three windows on the west wall there is a frieze depicting a Roman marriage. The four monochrome figures on the walls of the landing portray the arts, and the painting on the landing ceiling is a charming conceit, an oval window through which heavenly cherubs cast blessings upon all within the house.

Both the staircase and the 300-year-old frescoes at Reigate Priory are now in great need of restoration,

a very costly enterprise. A lottery bid is about to be made (1998) and we are cautiously optimistic. Who knows? they might even disclose a little painted porcupine, Verrio's symbolic signature.

When the cracked wall to the north of the Priory staircase was investigated in the 1980s and the traces of a medieval wall painting were found, another discovery was a broken seventeenth-century pottery bowl hidden between the joists under the old floor boards of the tiny room sealed by John Parsons' workmen.

By now the ancient religious house had become a gracious family home, already rich in important architectural features and in human history.

The Priory Estate

At the County Record Office at Kingston is a roughly drawn sketch map on an odd sheet of paper. This is the earliest plan of the Priory estate which has come to light. From the notes we can date it to the time of John Parsons, around 1700. The position of the grand new entrance is shown, with 'a coach way planted on each side'. Another avenue is shown running directly west to Park Lane, 'a walk lately planted across a mead'. We can see 'the Devil's Alehouse upon the Bank of Park Pond'. A spring and a watercourse are shown by the ponds, and a stable and ice house nearer the house. Out-buildings and horse ponds have been built at the west end of the Priory house. In the south east corner of 'The Park Hills' is a fenced-off area labelled 'The Spittle Field claimed by Mr Alderman Parsons. A Lodge now pulled down'. Spittlefield was a name usually used for land from which the rent went towards the upkeep of the hospital - so this was of ancient origin. In more recent times this became a sandpit, and then, appropriately, Sandhills Road. There are more little notes and drawings showing properties round the edge of the park.

Reigate in John Parsons' time

At that time the town of Reigate was quite small, and consisted of a line of small houses and shops, ale-houses and outbuildings each side of the High Street, and reaching a little way along West Street and Church Street, and down Park Lane and Bell Street. To the north were the remains of the old castle, which had been the stronghold of the Warennes, the Earls of Surrey. To the south was the

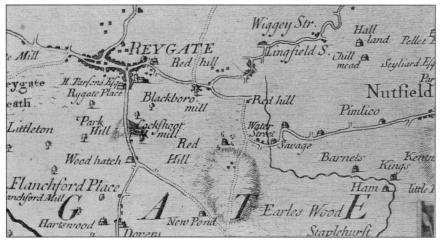

Reygate as shown in the John Senex map 1729. Note that Humphrey Parsons is mentioned by name and the house is called Rygate Place.

separate manor of the Priory.

Though small, Reigate was one of the four market towns in Surrey, so on Tuesdays and on fair days it was bustling with business. Though the local roads were notoriously bad, farmers brought in their produce from miles around. There was also a good trade in sand (for scouring and hourglasses), fullers' earth, local stone, charcoal and chalk. (It was at this time that the chalk scars were made on Reigate Hill and the deep hollows were created on the east side of Wray Lane). Pottery and bricks were made from the local clay. Hops and flax were grown here and there were the usual trades of brewing, black-smithing, shoe-making, etc.

Of particular interest to us, around twenty of the buildings were described as mills, and though we know there were two or three windmills then, most were driven by animal power. John Parsons was a

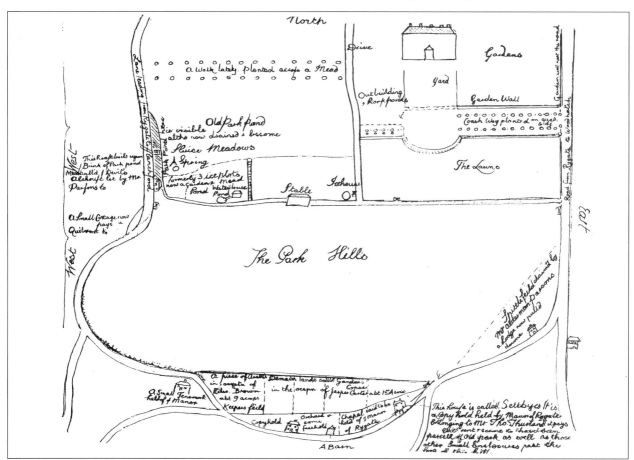

A rough sketch map – the earliest plan of the Priory estate.

victualler for the Navy; he was, in fact, made Commissioner for Victualling in 1683. Oatmeal was the chief ingredient for ship's biscuits, so it was John Parsons who promoted this trade in Reigate and encouraged the growing of oats by local farmers. Unfortunately, contractors for oatmeal often had to wait years for the payment of their accounts.

There is one very sad story about a certain Richard Rhodes, an oatmealman of Bell Street, who, on finding his housekeeper pregnant, murdered her, escaped to Ireland, was caught, tried and brought back to be hanged on the tree nearest the crime - which was a pear tree in his back garden. It came out at the trial that Sir John Parsons owed him £150 for oatmeal supplied to the Navy. A lot of money in those days!

John Parsons took a keen interest in local affairs. In the church, every Sunday morning just before the service started, there would be a great stir as the Priory contingent arrived, headed by **Sir** John Parsons - for he had been knighted by James II in 1687. We can imagine him arriving with great dignity, as befitted one of Reigate's Members of Parliament and owner of Reigate Priory, arrayed in a flamboyant befeathered hat, a wig of long curled hair, a skirted coat and embroidered waistcoat, and carrying a tall silver-topped cane. With him came his wife Elizabeth, his growing family of children and a retinue of twenty or thirty servants.

Church attendance had been enforced by law, so the church, though sizeable, was packed. It was not fitting for this important family to suffer any discomfort, so Sir John applied for a faculty which was granted to him to erect a gallery in the south

aisle, because 'he hath a fine house and estate within the Parish of Reigate, and a wife and several children and a very large family and has no pew belonging to him for them to kneel, pray, sit, stand and hear divine service and sermons'. This gallery was used by succeeding owners of the Priory for 150 years until it was removed in 1845.

It is interesting to remember that Sir John was a churchwarden and, as it says in the rules, 'Churchwardens are entrusted with the duty of providing seats for the parishioners'. I wonder if Sir John had to pay a pew rent. Perhaps not, for it is very likely that he himself paid for the gallery to be built. The yearly rent for a certain pew in the chancel at that time was half a guinea and a fat turkey!

The first public lending library

Vestry meetings at that time were sometimes held over the road at an inn - 'The Five Bells'. This was demolished later in the 18th Century when the house now called Cherchefelle was built. We can picture Sir John at the vestry meeting when the Vicar, the Rev Andrew Cranston, first mooted the idea of setting up a church library - not just for reference on site - but as a lending library.

The books were to be kept in the upper vestry. The Vicar would start off by donating about 70 of his own theological books. Then he hoped that offers would come of books or money to buy books - from local people in all walks of life and from friends all over the country. It wouldn't cost much. Russell, the local blacksmith, would give the bar and door fastenings and Henry Ware, the waggoner, wouldn't charge for carrying books. Mr Arnold would buy the book to keep the catalogue in, and Joseph Bostock, the writing master, would do the writing.

So in 1701, the Cranston Library was established. From the catalogue we learn that one of the early donors was 'the Worshipful Sir John Parsons of Reigate, Knight, Alderman and Citizen of London, and Member of Parliament for the said Borough of Reigate'. On November 23rd 1702 he donated 13 volumes (actually bound in 5 books) of Dupin's *Ecclesiastical History*. Then on July 15th the following year, there is an entry which I almost missed. There was a donation by **Henry** Parsons. This must have been Sir John's second son, 27 years old at the time. His contribution was not theological - it was Baptista Nani's *History of Venice*.

A view of the east end of Reigate Parish Church. In 1701 the Cranston Library was established in the upper vestry.

The names of many famous contemporaries of Sir John Parsons appear in the library catalogue -
The learned John Evelyn of Wootton;
The Rev. Mr. John Flamsteed, Rector of Burstow, 'the King's Mathematician';
Sir Richard Onslow of West Clandon and
The Earl of Shaftesbury.

Sir John actually used the library too! The catalogue lists not only donors, but borrowers. We discover that he did borrow back the books he had given, on December 20th 1711, and returned them on October 18th the following year.

Sir John Parsons, Lord Mayor of London

During all this time, Sir John Parsons was a very busy man. For in 1703, the first year of the reign of Queen Anne, he was elected to be Lord Mayor of London. Chosen by the people of the Portsoken Ward to be Alderman, by the members of his Livery Company to be Sheriff, by a committee of the top twelve Companies to be Lord Mayor, he had come through all the necessary steps to this high office. His original Company was, of course, the Brewers' Company (14th in rank), so to be eligible for Lord Mayor he transferred to the Fishmongers' Company, ranking fourth.

So, on September 29th 1703, from Alderman Parsons' Stairs, by the Brewery Wharf, he boarded the City of London Barge and proceeded to present himself to the Queen. The modern portrayal of this occasion is almost photographic. Sir John Parsons is proudly watched by his wife and his large family. His house-servants and brewery employees wave their master on his way. All the details of the City barge and the brewery are accurate.

Then, on October 29th, wearing the splendid scarlet Mayoral robes, and carrying the Sceptre, Seal, Purse and City Keys, Sir John Parsons proceeded in the City Barge, attended by the several Livery Companies in their respective barges, adorned with streamers and pennants, to be sworn in as Lord Mayor of London.

He is remembered chiefly for his generosity, for he gave up many of his official fees towards the payment of the City's debts, and for the relief of the poor and orphans.

The *London Gazette* records many of the functions he had to attend:-

'**November 5th, 1703** - A sermon was preached at St Paul's Cathedral before the Right Hon, the Lord Mayor and Court of Aldermen being the anniversary thanksgiving for our deliverance from the Gunpowder Plot.

'**January 19th, 1704** - A sermon was preached before the Rt.Hon the Lord Mayor, Aldermen and Citizens of London at the Cathedral Church of St Paul upon the occasion of the late dreadful storm and tempest and to implore the blessing of God in this present year.'

My favourite diarist John Evelyn vividly described that great storm, which had taken place on November 26th:-

'hurricane and tempest of wind, rain and lightening - many houses demolished and people killed - damage is almost tragical, not to be paralleled with anything happening in our age'.

We know that many trees in the Priory Park were blown over in this storm, as they were in **our** age in October 1987.

Another big event in John Parsons' mayoral year was the celebration for Marlborough's defeat of the French and Bavarians at Blenheim. Evelyn wrote 'This day was celebrated the thanksgiving for the late greate victory. The Lord Mayor, Sheriffs and Aldermen were in their scarlet robes, with caparison'd horses. At Temple Bar the Lord Mayor presented Her Majesty with the sword, which she returned. The great company proceeded to St Paul's.' We can picture these splendid occasions in Christopher Wren's masterpiece, the gleaming, newly built cathedral.

In Reigate Sir John Parsons celebrated his year in high office by presenting to the Parish Church a fine brass chandelier, with two tiers of eight branches for candles, a dove finial and coloured scrolling. It still hangs there in all its glory. The inscription around the globe reads 'The Gift of The Right Honourable Sir John Parsons, Knight 1704, then Lord Mayor of the City of London'. At the same time he fixed a similar, though smaller, chandelier over the staircase in the Priory, but unfortunately this disappeared in the 1940s and its present location is a discovery yet to be made.

The year of his mayoralty was, of course, the peak of Sir John's career, but he continued to serve Reigate as Member of Parliament until his death in 1717.

Not even at the Guildhall is there a portrait of Sir John Parsons, but in the Tower Hamlets library we tracked down documents carrying his signature.

Our Sir John Parsons trail finished where he was buried, at the church of St Botolph's, Aldgate, in the Portsoken Ward in which his London home and business were situated, and of which he was an Alderman.

High above the gallery, there is a splendid stained glass window in memory, not of John, but of his son Humphrey, who, strangely, is not buried at St Botolph's but at St Mary's, Reigate.

Humphrey Parsons

Humphrey made a remarkable achievement, for he became Lord Mayor of London not just once, but twice. Daniel Defoe foresaw this when he described his tour through Surrey in 1723. He wrote:

'Here travelling east at the foot of the hills, we came to Rygate, a large market-town with a castle, and a mansion-house, inhabited for some years by Sir John Parsons, once Lord Mayor of London, and whose son is in a fair way to be so also; being one

Alderman Humphrey Parsons – twice Lord Mayor of London.

of the aldermen and sheriffs of the said city at the writing of these sheets.'

When Sir John made his will in 1715 it was to Humphrey that he left 'all my manor house, commonly called the Priory, and my manor and tenement in the hamlet(!) of Reigate, in the county of Surrey - and all my lands, tenements, etc. in the town or parish of Epsom, also the Red Lion Brewhouse. . .'

Humphrey had inherited a flourishing business, an impressive country house and stables at Epsom and Reigate. His father before him had been very successful with his race-horses. Sir John had bred the famous Reigate Mare, and a horse called Plowman which had won the Prince's Plate at Newmarket. Now Humphrey could continue to breed, not only racing horses, but hunters. Humphrey was a keen huntsman and Master of the Hunt which used Epping Forest. He also hunted at Windsor and took his horses to France. On one occasion when in France he reached the kill before Louis XV. The King admired Humphrey's horse and asked him to put a price on it. Humphrey tactfully replied that the animal was 'beyond any price other than the king's acceptance'. The horse was accepted and from that time Humphrey enjoyed the king's friendship and generosity.

In 1719, two years after his father's death, he married Sarah, the daughter of Sir Ambrose Crowley of Greenwich. His wife brought him extra wealth and obviously had flamboyant tastes. She achieved notoriety on one occasion by causing annoyance to the Queen. Her Majesty had been offered some very beautiful silk brocade, but refused to purchase this when she learned its price - £50 a yard. Sarah Parsons, upon hearing of this, purchased the material and commissioned a full-length portrait of herself in the dress made of this sumptuous fabric. The Queen is said to have made a very sarcastic remark concerning a certain wealthy brewer's wife.

Here in Reigate Humphrey entertained lavishly at the Priory. Besides his being influential and wealthy, Humphrey's charismatic personality contributed to his success in business, civic and parliamentary life - he became MP for Harwich. Throughout these years he also took an active part in local Reigate life and, like his father, took seriously his responsibilities as a churchwarden.

His home at Reigate Priory was now ideal for entertaining. When he was created Master of the

Merchants of the Staple of England, this prestigious company feasted here in grand style. His hospitality extended to many other companies and to people from the highest levels of society. He used his influence to procure talented entertainers for his guests, in at least one case, from a very unlikely source:

John Baptist Grano visits the Priory

A visitor to the Priory Museum, John Ginger, told us of a fascinating diary which he had discovered at Oxford. It is *The Prison Diary of John Baptist Grano*, and we actually held it in our hands when we visited the Bodleian Library.

Grano, in his mid-30s, was imprisoned in the Marshalsea at Southwark for running up debts of £99. Evidently Grano had a considerable musical talent; he composed and he played the trumpet and the flute. He had even played in Handel's orchestra. Our wealthy brewer must have approached the prison governor, Mr Acton, to allow Grano, for a fee of five shillings, to go out under escort and to perform on special occasions. The escort was usually the Governor himself, who obviously enjoyed some good days out too!

The diary gives us vivid first-hand accounts of the life of the time. One page describes how he was summoned by Alderman Humphrey Parsons to perform on Lord Mayor's Day 1728. At that time, Humphrey was Master of the Grocers' Livery Company.

Obviously John Grano gave satisfaction, for in the following year he was invited to come down to Reigate, where there was to be a firework display and a musical entertainment. On this occasion he came without his prison governor, and lodged at the Greyhound Inn, beside the wide castle steps, in Reigate High Street.

'**Tuesday morn, the 5th of August.** Made a shift to get into Reigate before twelve and put up at the Greyhound, then dressed and went to the Alderman's where in about half-an-hour dinner came on the table. After dinner I went into the garden and sounded about 24 airs, after which came in-a-doors and had the honour of drinking tea with the ladies, namely Madam Parsons and Miss Cotton. In the evening there was fireworks, and then I gave a tune or two on my trumpet.'

Grano records in his diary that he went back to his inn and, as he went to bed, the clock struck one in the morning.

'**Wednesday morn, the 6th of August.** Got up about seven, went into the yard and stables, fed the horse with corn, took a turn up a hill behind our inn, came back and performed a spiritual exercise, then shaved, amused myself about the yard and next the street till a shirt was prepared for me. When dressed, went to the Alderman's where I drank tea, sounded a tune or two; after which, the hours being about ten, went into the coach, where with the Alderman we came safe as far as Vauxhall without any sort of accident, where we took boat. We landed at the nearest stairs to Exchange Alley, went directly to the Swan, where the Alderman gave me a very good dinner, some of his own small beer and burgundy.'

Of course his 'turn up the hill behind our inn' must have been a stroll up into what is now the Castle Grounds.

The following week we find Grano actually staying at the Priory, for the birthday celebrations of Humphrey's only surviving son, John - who later squandered the family fortunes. Grano describes how he arrived tired and dishevelled, so he had a rest in the 'diminutive room' which had been allotted to him, before he came down and performed for the family and guests. He 'piped company' and he danced until four in the morning. So, next day …

'**Thursday morn, the 14th of August.** Awoke as the house clocks struck nine; got up at ten, went downstairs into the parlour where French Peter (one of the Alderman's servants) was so good to shave me, powder my wig, etc. After which, took a turn into the garden where, being alone, made an extempore prayer etc. Returned into the house between eleven and twelve o'clock, where in the hall perceived several ladies waiting for Madam Parsons' arrival downstairs to have some breakfast; and to amuse the time they accepted of my performance in the great staircase on the German flute. When breakfast was over I went into the garden where I sounded a few airs and after that stepped into Reigate town where I called at Counsellor Bonnick's to ask him a lawful question; but was told he was gone up Redhill, a mountain (!) somewhere in the neighbourhood. The next morning …

'**Friday morn, the 15th of August**. Got up about 9, had the honour of drinking tea and eating bread and butter with the ladies, went to chapel and heard prayers with Madam Parsons and two of Sir John Hind Cotton's sisters.

'That night, the Alderman was so good to his servants as to give them liquor and a fiddle, with leave to drink and dance as long as they thought proper.

'After supper we sat till 12, then we broke up and I went directly to bed, in very good health, thank God.'

The name Hynde (or Hind) Cotton occurs frequently in the diary. Madam Parsons' sister Lettice had married Sir John Hynde Cotton, 4th baronet - and Humphrey and Sarah's daughter Ann, aged only 15 or 16, was to marry their son, her cousin, who became Sir John Hynde Cotton, 5th baronet. This connection led to our most recent and most exciting discoveries. These are so recent, that they must appear as a postscript to this chapter.

The diary finishes Tuesday 23rd September, 1729. I wonder! Did Humphrey help John Grano to pay off his debts? Did John Grano take part in the celebrations the following year, when Humphrey became, like his father before him, Lord Mayor of London?

Twice Lord Mayor of London

That year of office must have been a triumph. His popularity was so great that he was elected a second time, ten years later. This Lord Mayor's Show of 1740 is recorded as being of unusual splendour, for Humphrey Parsons was the first Lord Mayor to ride in a magnificent gilded coach, drawn by six splendid horses, gaily decorated in trappings, and with four elaborately dressed footmen behind. An engraving by William Hogarth shows the scene - with stands erected for the spectators (one has collapsed!) and soldiers firing a salute. The procession is being watched from a balcony by the Prince and Princess of Wales.

The river procession too was more splendid than ever. I wonder whether John Grano was blowing away on this occasion, perhaps a performance of Handel's *Water Music?*

Unfortunately this second term of office lasted only six months, for Humphrey died suddenly at the Hermitage on 21st March 1741 aged 65. He

William Hogarth's 'satirical print' of the Lord Mayor's show in 1740.

had asked for a simple funeral, but it became a grand civic occasion, perhaps the most spectacular event which has ever occurred in Reigate Parish Church.

For, as we have noted, he was not buried at St Botolph's, the official resting place for Aldermen of his Ward, but, in accordance with his wishes, in the Priory vault at St Mary's, where three of his children lay. The *Daily Post*, April 4th 1741, says 'The corpse of the late Right Hon Humphrey Parsons, after laying in state at his country seat, was magnificently deposited in the Family Vault at Reigate, the trophies of the Praetorial Office being carried in procession'.

The final verses of a *Hymn to Alderman Parsons, our Lord Mayor* sum up the qualities of both father and son, though actually written about Humphrey in 1730.

'He is a loyal Churchman, and for our Rights will stand,
He fears no Presbyterian that worketh underhand,
No courtier e'er can bribe him, he always will be just,
He'll take no bribe nor pension for to betray his trust,
But is in every action a loyal worthy soul,
Then to our Lord Mayor Parsons, toss off a flowing bowl.

His father's noble actions he strives to imitate,
Altho' he's but a brewer, he is both good and great,
He fears no treacherous enemies, nor loves no fawning friends,
Nor will he stain his honour, for any private ends.
Long may he live, and brew good beer, to cheer each honest heart,
So to his health let each true soul toss off a bumper quart.'

The Red Lion Brewery continued brewing for two more centuries but finally closed in 1936 - so Parsons' Black Champagne is now just a legend.

Postscript - A new find of Information

We have already mentioned Ann Parsons who married the younger John Hynde Cotton. As the wife of the fifth baronet Ann became the mistress of Madingley Hall near Cambridge. In time, Ann inherited from her father a share of the Priory properties.

These estate papers are lodged at the Cambridge County Record Office and provide a source of information hitherto unexplored by Priory historians. We found them by following up a pencilled note in Ernest Scears' notebook.

Among the Cotton papers there are at least 24 documents which relate to Reigate and the Priory. Many of these deal with estate properties, and one of these of particular interest concerns a footpath across Humphrey Parsons' land, 'near his engine and ice houses'. The engine house would contain the pumps to supply water to the house. There are also handwritten inventories of plate and of Madam Parsons' Toilet.

But to me, the most interesting is the earliest, dated 1495. It is a lease for 40 years of 60 acres on Reigate Hill, with free warren. It was granted by Prior Alexander Shott to the Lords of the Manor of Reigate, Thomas, Duke of Norfolk and Thomas, Earl of Derby, and the annual rent was a red rose! At least half survives of the red wax seal about 1¼ inches in diameter, showing the Holy Cross on one side and W (for Warenne) on the reverse.

There is a magic about seeing and handling an original object or document, particularly one which makes a link spanning five centuries. No time machine is needed, just a flash of imagination.

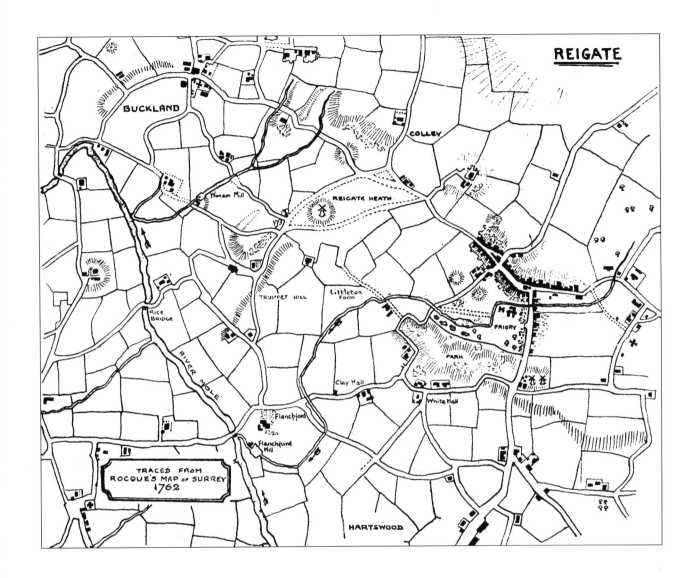

REIGATE

BUCKLAND

COLLEY

Nonam Mill

REIGATE HEATH

TRUMPET HILL

Littleton Farm

RICE BRIDGE

RIVER MOLE

PARK

PRIORY

Clay Hall

White Hall

Flanchford

Flanchford Mill

TRACED FROM
ROCQUE'S MAP OF SURREY
1762

HARTSWOOD

DISCOVERING RICHARD IRELAND AND GEORGE MOWBRAY

T he next two owners of Reigate Priory were gentlemen who were little known in their day, or ours. As people they remain enigmatic, but discoveries which came to light in the early 1980s revealed new, detailed information which explains some features of the park and the building for which these two men were responsible.

'Miserable old cheesemonger'. That is how William Ridgeway, his contemporary, described Richard Ireland in a manuscript history of Reigate, which is in the Cranston library.

Richard Ireland comes into the Priory story in 1766, when there was an interesting sale by auction at the Devil Tavern, Temple Bar in London. Lot 1 was 'The Manor, Capital Messuage and late dissolved Priory of Reigate'. The best bidder was Richard Ireland, who paid £4,000 for the Priory mansion and 76 acres of parkland. He bought the furniture at a valuation.

What did Richard Ireland buy?

One Wednesday afternoon in 1983 Mr Gammon of Merstham, a visitor to the museum, brought for us a large folded map, meticulously drawn and painted on paper, backed with linen. This had been found by a friend of his, a Mr Muddiman, in an old trunk in his attic. This thrilling acquisition is reproduced in full colour in this book.

The title declares it to be a Survey of the Priory and Lands adjoining in the Parish of Reigate and County of Surrey Belonging to Rich. Ireland Esq. No date is given. The Table showing the land usage and the calculations of value which are written roughly on the back suggest that Ireland was reckoning up his new assets.

This survey, executed with much care and skill, shows the shape and extent of the Priory buildings with the east and west wings at full length, just as they were when William Howard had demolished the southern range of buildings in the sixteenth century. The coach houses, the stables and the horse ponds are shown. The lawn at the east end, still there today, was at that time used as a bowling green. To the north there were the 'cheery' orchard and the kitchen gardens bordered by a wavy line which could be the stream, utilised for irrigation as in the past. The ancient fish-ponds are shown, all six of them with their interesting shapes. We recognise the ice house, from the earlier sketch map, and we can see the position of the grand new eagle gateway from Bell Street, created by the Parsons. Just to the north of it is a tiny lodge, the ogee-shaped doorway to which remains today and was restored a few years ago. As in John Parsons' sketch map, the way to the Devil's Alehouse seems rather important! This map of the Priory estate is most valuable, for it tells us more than pages of words.

But all we know about Ireland himself is that he was 66 years of age at this time, a bachelor and wealthy. For some time he had owned Kinnersley Manor, about three miles south of Reigate, but was then living in the Glebe House at Dorking, a large property rented from the Parsons, now lot 11 in the sale.

John Wesley visits the Priory

Ireland's sister Ann, with her husband Thomas Fisher and their daughter Ann, lived in Dorking too. For some time the Fishers had been very active nonconformists. When John Wesley, the celebrated travelling preacher and founder of

John Wesley, founder of Methodism.

Methodism, visited Dorking in 1764, he met Richard Ireland, and it was this encounter which must have led to an invitation six years later. For in his Diary for Wednesday 19th December 1770, Wesley wrote 'About noon I preached at Dorking, the hearers were many and seemed all attentive. About an hundred attended at Reigate in the evening and between 20 and 30 in the morning. Dull, indeed, as stones!'

Almost a year later, on Tuesday December 17th 1771, Wesley was in Reigate again, referring to the Priory as Reigate Place. He wrote in his Diary - 'In King Henry IV's time this had been an eminent monastery … The gentleman who possesses it now has entirely changed the form of it, pulling down whole piles of ancient buildings and greatly altering what remains. Yet, after all is taken away, it still looked more like a palace than a private house. The staircase is of the same model with that at Hampton Court … the chimney piece in the hall is probably one of the most curious pieces of woodwork in this kingdom. I preached in the evening to a small company - all seemed moved for the present.'

Richard Ireland's changes to the Priory

So we learn that the Priory had undergone great changes under its new owner. Rocque's map shows the shape of the building and estate very clearly as they had been in 1762, but the survey rescued by Mr Gammon shows us the estate in far more detail, soon after it was purchased by Richard Ireland. Wesley's diary tells us that the changes were made by 1771 and we know the reason - there was a devastating fire in the west wing of the old cloister. Instead of repairing and restoring it, Ireland shortened the east wing to match - from 75 feet to 25 feet. The height of the walls was increased by seven or eight feet to match the main building, and a new slated roof was put on, not so steep as the old roof, replacing the old Horsham slabs. The Tudor stone mullioned windows were removed, all but one, and replaced by the Georgian sash windows we can see today. The whole south front, built 500 years earlier of Reigate stone must, by this time, have been badly weathered, and it was completely refaced with cement stucco.

The H-shaped gatehouse, 70 feet or so west of the main Priory building, had been completely removed by the time of the survey. Foundations of the demolished sections of the old cloisters and of the great gatehouse are still buried a few feet down - but we have glimpses sometimes when they are uncovered by workmen or gardeners.

The old north-west porch and the projection at the north east end of the church, probably originally a side chapel, were joined up by a brick wall from ground to roof level. This created extra rooms on both floors.

What happened to all those other stone window

South view of Reigate Priory, before Ireland's alterations.

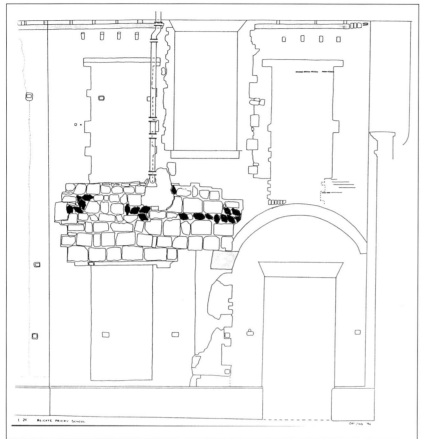

A historical jigsaw. The west-facing wall was uncovered in 1996. The stones marked in black are mullion fragments.

had obviously been reconstructed and altered on various occasions, but earlier material had been re-used. There was Reigate stonework again, there was a stone archway, now blocked. At the higher levels there were rows of bricks. To fill in odd spaces there were shaped pieces of stone, recognisable as fragments of those Tudor mullioned windows! A historical jigsaw.

Richard Ireland died at the Priory on January 9th 1780. Though little known in Reigate, he certainly left his mark on the Priory, and he was buried, with the Howards and the Parsons, under the chancel of the Parish Church in the Priory vault.

A letter survives from John Wesley to Richard Ireland written on April 25th 1777, inviting him to subscribe towards the building of his 'New Chapel' in City Road, London. Mr Ireland did not respond so it appears that Wesley failed to move the 'miserable old cheesemonger' permanently. In a later diary entry, he mentions Ireland with sadness as being 'poor beyond expression, though he left fourscore thousand pounds behind him'.

frames and the lumps of Reigate stone from those demolished buildings? We are beginning to find out - after two centuries. One day in 1982, a couple of workmen, who were repairing the Priory's 18th century perimeter wall fronting Bell Street, staggered in with a massive stone they had found incorporated in the foundations. This was unmistakably a complete section from one of the stone-mullioned windows discarded by Richard Ireland. It matches exactly the cross-piece of the only surviving example which remains in situ today, upstairs beside the staircase to the so-called 'Monk's Room' - but in a position where it would have overlooked the courtyard, before Richard Ireland's brick joining wall was constructed.

In the early 1980s, in the course of repairs to the rendering on the east-facing wall of the old Lady Chapel, large areas of the original Priory wall were uncovered - row upon row of Reigate stone blocks.

More recently, in 1996, at the west end, the walls of the old north porch had to be stripped. These walls

The Joneses

The Priory and the fortune were left to Richard Ireland's niece Ann Jones, the daughter of his sister Ann Fisher of Dorking. First Ann Jones, then later, her son Arthur Jones, lived at the Priory for many years.

Ann had 13 children and her son Arthur had ten. The dates of their births, baptisms and deaths, many of them at the Priory, are recorded in a perfectly preserved family Bible which is still treasured by their descendants. Many of those children died very young, most of them from smallpox - the scourge of that time. Arthur and his wife Sarah courageously invited Dr Jenner to inoculate their later children - most of whom survived.

Some present-day members of this family visit the Priory on occasion. But after the Ireland and later Jones ownership of the Priory ended in 1801, our information is thin.

George Mowbray

For seven years we have little but a name - George Mowbray! Until fairly recently we knew nothing about this man and the development of the building under his ownership.

On a Wednesday afternoon in February 1981 a retired London architect, Dr William Bonwitt, came from Chelsea to share with us his recent discovery. In the course of his research in the R.I.B.A. library he had come across a drawing labelled:-

Intended Elevation, West Front of Reigate Priory for Geo. Mowbray Esq.by M Searles 1802.

This showed us the handsome classical design for the modernisation of the Priory's West wall - the location of the original Great West Door.

Dr Bonwitt told us that Michael Searles lived in Southwark and had built houses in various parts of London. Also he had designed Woodhatch House, less than a mile away from the Priory, as a new country home for Rees Price, a wealthy Southwark hop factor. Perhaps Price recommended this architect to his new neighbour at Reigate Priory - George Mowbray.

As we look at the Priory's west elevation today, we still see the arched landing windows and the pediment, remnants of Searles' handsome design. The pillars supporting the pediment have been removed. Many Victorian prints, paintings and maps show the great two-storey bay windows, but no sign of them remains today. The later addition of the Library and the extension of the drawing room have unfortunately wrecked the elegance of Searles' design. Is it possible that Searles' design was not carried out exactly as intended, but was adapted to include the structure which became the library? John Hassell's water-colour drawing of 1824 shows a building extending from the old Great West Door much earlier than 1850, the date which is usually given for the library.

Why did George Mowbray buy Reigate Priory and keep it for so short a time - 1801 to 1807? The question challenged us. How could we learn more about Mowbray? At least we could look at the sale documents lodged with the Somers papers at the County Records Office in Kingston.

A morning's search revealed a few clues. The first document, dated 8th September 1801, revealed that George Mowbray, of Devonshire Street, Portland Place, Middlesex, started by arranging a lease for one year of 'that capital messuage or manor house called or known by the name of the Priory House or Place House situate or standing and being at Reigate aforesaid in the said County of Surrey and also all barns, stables, dovehouses, courtyards, gardens, orchard lands, water ponds pools, priviledged profits, commodities and appurtenances whatsoever to the capital messuage and all those lands and grounds called the lawns, now in the occupation of the said Arthur Jones and his undertenants and also that piece or parcel of arable and woodland, now or late called by the name of Spital Field, situate in Reigate, heretofore in the tenure and occupation of Thomas Holdsworth, now in the occupation of the said Arthur Jones … etc.' This quaint legal wording appears with the appropriate name changes in the Priory transactions over two or three centuries.

Next we learned that on 9th September 1801 (the next day) at a public auction held at Carraway's Coffee House, Cornhill, Reigate Priory was sold in two lots, for £8,350, to George Mowbray.

A further discovery was a document dated 23rd December 1807, only six years later, setting out the articles of purchase of the Priory between George Mowbray and John, Lord Somers, who was already Lord of the Manor of Reigate.

The price had almost doubled - £16,000, and the furniture came extra - £3,242 - 7s - 6d. The Priory

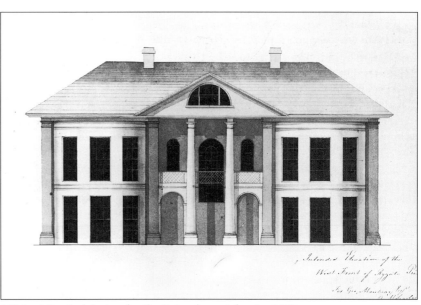

Michael Searles' design for the Priory's west front – 1802.

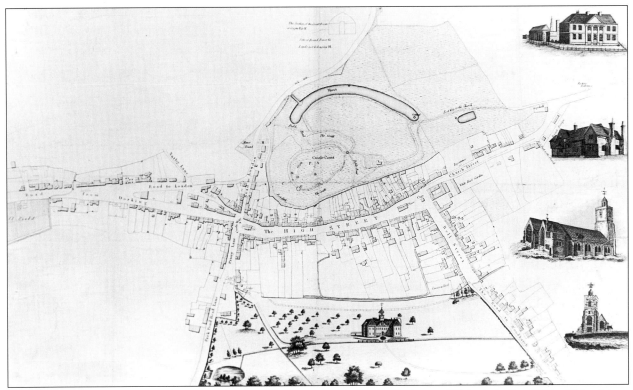

An artist's view of the Priory (inaccurately placed!) shown in relation to the town of Reigate in the 1780s. This picture appears in a unique edition of Manning and Bray's History and Antiquities of the County of Surrey.

historian Ernest Scears held the view that Mowbray merely held the Priory on behalf of John Somers, but the purchase and sale details show that the deal brought him a very good profit.

So could it be that George Mowbray recognised that John Somers was a highly ambitious man who would value the opportunity to reunite the Priory sub-manor with the manor of Reigate, which in due course he would inherit. The added votes would consolidate the Somers majority and make sure of the parliamentary seat. The ownership of this pleasant country home and estate near London would enhance his chances of social and political advancement and he might be willing to pay a good price for these privileges. We get the strong impression that Mowbray was a canny businessman.

Our last glimpse of George Mowbray told us that he died in May 1825 and his executors were named Cockburn and Turin.

Many questions remain unanswered, but new information is constantly emerging, some of it hunted down and some, like the survey and the architect's drawing, turning up at the Priory out of the blue.

In 1697 William III granted Lord Chancellor Somers the 'Manors of Reygate and Howleigh, in Surrey, together with an annuity of £2100 out of the fee-farm rents'. At that time Sir John Parsons owned the Priory manor and would have had many dealings with Lord Somers' trustee Sir Joseph Jekyll. Through these two families the two manors of the town and the Priory were eventually re-united in December 1807.

THE SOMERS FAMILY - A LORD CHANCELLOR AND THREE EARLS

S ome of the most useful clues to a town's history are its street names. Here in Reigate we have Somers Road, Hardwicke Road, Yorke Road, Worcester Road, Ledbury Road, Evesham Road, Beaufort Road and St Albans Road. In the South Park area, as well as Priory Road, there is Eastnor Road. In Meadvale, there is Somerset Road. These owe their names to the family which for 224 years owned the Manor of Reigate and for 113 years the Priory Manor too - the Somers family.

Chancellor Somers and the Manor of Reigate

To understand the Somers connection we have to go back to 1697, to a man who, by all accounts, was almost too good to be true. 'A young lawyer of extraordinary merit' wrote John Evelyn in his diary. Macaulay, always biassed in favour of Whigs, described him extravagantly as 'one of those divine men who, like a chapel in a palace, remain unprofaned, while all the rest is tyranny, corruption and folly.' He was 'the most uncorrupt lawyer and the honestest statesman, a master orator and a genius of fine taste'. 'He was equally eminent as a jurist and as a politician. He acquired the authority of an oracle'.

This paragon was John Somers - sometimes spelt Sommers. He was born in Worcester in 1650, educated at Trinity College, Oxford, and called to the bar in 1676. Both as a lawyer and as a politician, his speeches were brief, powerful and persuasive and it was clear that he had the soundest judgement of anyone in the Whig party.

The king, William III, came to value John Somers so highly that he appointed him first to be Solicitor General, next Attorney General, then Keeper of the Great Seal. In 1697 Somers was appointed Lord High Chancellor of England and the king conferred upon him the title of Baron Somers of Evesham.

To support this high office, the king granted to John Somers the Manors of Reigate and Hooley, to be held in trust for him by his sister's husband, Joseph Jekyll.

Joseph Jekyll - trustee

As trustee for the new Lord of the Manor of Reigate, Joseph Jekyll took an active part in Reigate affairs. Although Reigate Priory was a separate manor, he must have had many dealings with its owner at that time, the wealthy brewer Sir John Parsons.

In parliamentary elections they would have supported opposite sides, for Parsons was a staunch Tory and Jekyll an equally staunch Whig. For many years Sir John Parsons and his eldest son

Reigate's Market and Sessions House upon ten arches in 1837, looking eastwards towards the White Hart in Bell Street.

John held the Reigate seats, but from 1722 it was Sir Joseph Jekyll and his party who held the seats for sixteen years.

A local enterprise supported by both of them was the Parish Library, founded, as already mentioned, by the vicar, Rev Andrew Cranston, in 1701. When Cranston died in 1708 a body of 44 trustees was formed to ensure its preservation. These included, naturally, Reigate's leading personalities, Sir Joseph Jekyll and Sir John Parsons. We still cherish the Cranston Library, the first public lending library in England, as a local and national treasure.

When the great Chancellor Somers died unmarried in 1716, his heirs were his two sisters, Elizabeth, who had married Joseph Jekyll and Mary, the elder, who married Charles Cocks, M.P. for Worcester. It was Jekyll, in 1728, who replaced the old chapel of Thomas à Becket, in the market place, with the 'Market and Sessions House upon ten arches', which marks the centre of Reigate today, and is known to us as the Old Town Hall.

Mary and Charles Cocks' daughter Margaret married Philip Yorke, who was later created Earl of Hardwicke. These names, Yorke and Hardwicke, became closely linked with that of Somers, for a long period of Reigate's history.

Mary's grandson, also named Charles Cocks, had inherited the substantial Somers fortune and the recreated Somers Barony. It is his son, John Cocks, Baron Somers, who brings us back to the story of Reigate Priory.

The First Earl Somers

John Cocks was born in 1760, in turn inheriting the Somers wealth and properties. His marriage to Margaret, daughter of Dr Treadway Nash, almost doubled his resources. He was capable and relentlessly ambitious. He became Lord Lieutenant of Herefordshire, High Steward of Hereford and Recorder of Gloucester.

For many years, Reigate's two seats in Parliament were held by a representative of each of the two families, Somers and Hardwicke. The Somers family, who already held the manor of Reigate, was now trying to acquire the Priory, mainly, we suspect, to increase their holding of parliamentary votes. The detailed survey undertaken in 1786 by William Bryant, son of Reigate's bailiff, had revealed that the Somers majority over the Hardwicke faction was, to say the

John Cocks, Baron Somers, inherited the manor of Reigate in 1806 and bought Reigate Priory from George Mowbray in 1807 at the age of 47.

least, questionable. The purchase of the Priory on 23rd December, 1807 removed any doubts (as we have seen - at a price).

John became Lord of the re-united Manors of Reigate and Reigate Priory, and this was confirmed by a special Act of Parliament. He now had a comfortable mansion, conveniently near London, and a safe majority for the seat he owned in the 'pocket borough' of Reigate. The family's main home was the manor house of Castleditch at Eastnor, near the charming little town of Ledbury, close to the Malvern Hills. Lord Somers decided to replace the old house and employed Sir Robert Smirke to design an imposing baronial pile, Eastnor Castle. Building started in 1812. He had become a man of some substance, so in 1821 he was raised to the titles of Earl Somers and Viscount Eastnor.

That brings our score for Somers-linked street names to eight!

When Margaret his first wife died in 1834, he married his cousin Jane, a daughter of James Cocks. His worldly success did not however extend

An engraving commissioned by Lord Somers showing his new country seat.

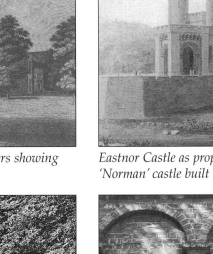

Eastnor Castle as proposed by the architect, effectively a 'Norman' castle built in 1812!

John, Earl Somers' tunnel built in 1823...

... and the inscription to his memory.

to his private life. As we read in the recent guide book to Eastnor Castle -

'He married twice, but both wives fled
Unable to stand the man they wed.'

Meanwhile, the death of his eldest son and heir had dealt the family a great blow. Edward Charles Cocks, MP for Reigate in 1806-7 and then an Intelligence Officer in the Peninsular War, was killed at the Battle of Burgos in 1812.

The first road tunnel in England

The Earl was a generous benefactor to Reigate. In 1819 he and Lord Hardwicke gave Reigate its first two fire-fighting appliances.

But his best gift was the Tunnel. In his day the notoriously bad local roads were being transformed by the Turnpike Trusts. Travel by coach or carriage was becoming safer and faster, and from Reigate people could comfortably get up to London or down to Brighton, for their business or pleasure.

Unfortunately, Reigate's road system involved two sharp bends to get round the castle grounds into the High Street, and then to turn south from the market place.

Earl Somers had an inspirational idea, a tunnel cut through the sandstone obstruction on which the Warennes had built their castle 700 years earlier. William Constable, the surveyor who was straightening and lowering the road over Reigate Hill, also undertook this amazing engineering feat, which is now considered to be the first road tunnel in England.

Cobbett, in his *Rural Rides*, thought it was a disgraceful misuse of money, but most travellers appreciated the new, shorter, direct route. Their carriages could bowl merrily down Reigate Hill, stopping only to pay sixpence at the two toll gates, one at the Yew Tree Inn, the other at the south end of the tunnel. Then straight past the market place to the White Hart, which for centuries stood in Bell Street and was the most popular coaching stop on the old London to Brighton Road.

In our time, the tunnel is pedestrianised, so it is quite safe to stop, look up and read the tribute to John, the first Earl Somers, who in 1823 gave Reigate a short cut which is now a distinctive feature of the town.

Another welcome improvement had come just a little earlier, in 1815, when the Wray stream, which had crossed Bell Street near the Priory entrance, was culverted.

The first Earl Somers encouraged another local amenity for the farmers and townspeople. He made part of Reigate Heath available for a racecourse, where race meetings were held each year from 1834 to 1838, then again in 1863 and 1864. Eventually these were abandoned, partly because they did not pay and partly because they attracted a rough element to the town.

The Second Earl Somers

By 1842 when yet another John succeeded as the second Earl Somers, the family had obtained a licence to use the surname Somers Cocks. In contemporary documents we find that he also used a distinctive squiggle above the 'm' of Somers, perhaps a reference to the extra 'm' of the alternative spelling.

Before succeeding, the younger John had been M.P. for Reigate from 1812 to 1818, and again from 1832 to 1841. In the years between, he was M.P. for Hereford.

It was he who gave the land for St John's Church and schools. Following family tradition he made generous contributions towards the restoration of Reigate Parish Church and attended services regularly.

In 1815 he had married Lady Caroline Yorke, the youngest daughter of the third Earl of Hardwicke - the second link with this family. They lived at Reigate Priory for most of their married life, and on 14th July 1819 their first son, Charles, was born. (I wonder, was Dr Thomas Martin, the brilliant

young practitioner just across the road in Bell Street, summoned to be present for the birth?).

The Third Earl Somers

Though Charles Somers Cocks held the impressive title of Viscount Eastnor, he was not an impressive figure, but when he inherited the Somers earldom in 1852, he already had a stunningly beautiful wife. Their first little daughter was already showing signs of strong character and her story will be told in the next chapter.

For a few years the Earl was Lord in Waiting to Queen Victoria, but most of his official responsibilities reflected his chief interest. In his youth, when he expressed his wish to be a painter, his mother witheringly remarked, 'as a member of the aristocracy, you can only paint badly'. As we shall discover, he obviously pursued his urge to paint - not badly either. He became a Trustee of the Portrait Gallery and of the British Museum. Charles Somers greatly enjoyed the new hobby of photography - this was acceptable - and became Vice-President of the Photographic Society of London.

Reigate in the Third Earl's time

It was during Charles Somers' ownership of the Priory that Reigate developed and expanded so rapidly. The London to Brighton railway had opened in 1841 and the cross line running through Reigate opened in 1849. Between 1801 and 1861, with better communications, the population of Reigate parish had shot up from around 2,500 to 10,000, so land was needed for houses, churches and schools. Essential services had to be provided - a water supply, a gas supply and a sewerage system. A police force and a fire service were needed. Improved provision was needed for the

'Redhill and Reigate' Station in 1856.

sick and for the poor.

The second and third earls, following tradition, supported many of these enterprises by giving land, by waiving mineral rights, and by guaranteeing free use, particularly of the commons. It was the third Earl who generously opened the Castle Grounds and Reigate Park for public enjoyment.

Dr Thomas Martin, one of the most loved and respected personalities in Reigate's history, had his home and medical practice in Bell Street, just opposite to the Priory, and he attended the Somers family when they were in residence here. Dr Martin must have had close dealings with each of the Earls Somers, for he was not only a brilliant and energetic medical practitioner with a deep concern for public health, but also Reigate's high bailiff and the Somers were, after all, Lords of the Manor. Dr Martin initiated most of the local projects to improve living standards. He founded dispensaries, a cottage gardeners' society, a savings bank, a Mechanics' Institute and two or three local schools. He publicised the dangers of smoking and drinking.

When in 1859 local people petitioned for the establishment of a municipal borough, the Lord of the Manor was less than enthusiastic. It was Dr Martin who presented to Earl Somers the petition which led to the creation of our Borough. In March 1863 a public enquiry was held. The Commissioner uncovered a chaotic situation - 17 different, uncoordinated authorities in the parish. In December 1863, 18 councillors, six aldermen and a mayor were elected. The old 'boroughs' of Santon, Colley, Woodhatch, Linkfield, Hooley and Reigate joined to become the Municipal Borough of Reigate.

The background of the Borough badge and seal consisted of the blue and gold chequers of the great Warenne family. There were crosses representing Reigate Priory, but unfortunately these were omitted in the new Borough badge of 1974.

Dr Thomas Martin died in 1867 and his personal papers are now lodged in the Surrey Record Office. They include the original petition for a municipal borough, which carries many names of families still active in Reigate today. There are many other books and papers in the Record Office which fill in the details of life in Reigate and at the Priory during the Somers ownership.

There is for example a Priory account book. Each entry could provide a scenario for an episode in a historical film. For example:

28. 2. 1853 - to Westwood, 15 yds of staircarpet	£1 - 7s - 6d.	
1853 - Cygnets - recd. on sale of a pair	£2 - 2s - 0d.	
advertisement	6s - 0d.	
catching	1s - 0d.	
Nichols, poulterer	4s - 0d.	
7. 1. 1854 - paid 10 men getting ice and filling ice-house and for bread and cheese and beer for the men	£2 - 1s - 2d.	
18. 2. 1856 - one load and a half of straw for new thatching the ice-house	£2 - 5s - 0d.	
27. 2. 1856 - to James Briggs, his Bill for Garden Seeds for Priory Gardens	£2 - 4s - 9d.	
24. 2. 1857 - to James Fisher, glazing and gilding bookcases, framing pictures, cleaning and colouring storeroom and bedroom ceilings and other work	£25 - 13s - 8d.	
1857 - Priory Gardens - recd. of Matthews for celery sold	£1 - 4s - 3d.	
asparagus.	£5 - 13s - 9d.	
5. 7. 1858 - to Mrs Harrison [the vicar's wife] for 30 mourning bonnets for the National School Children on occasion of the death of the late Earl	£5 - 7s - 4d.	

Notice the date of this last item - the second Earl died in 1852!

8. 7. 1858 - to Martin and Holman Their bill for medical attendance in 1856 (!) . . .	£24 - 0s - 6d.	

Sections of this account book are reserved for recording money received from letting Reigate Priory when the family was not in residence. These will tell their own story later.

There are other account books dealing with the rents and expenses concerning the Somers' manorial properties. For many years the estate business was transacted in a room at the Swan Inn in the High Street - then later at the Old Town Hall.

Charles the collector

In fact, Charles, the third earl, a sensitive man with delicate health, did not enjoy his responsibilities as a property owner. He was a connoisseur of art in

A bad attack of 'armoritis' at Eastnor Castle.

many forms, his friends were artists, poets and writers. At Eastnor he laid out the grounds as an arboretum second only to that at Westonbirt, created by his friend and travelling companion Mr Holford. With help from his artist friend, G F Watts, he transformed the interior, acquiring exquisite furniture, pictures, sculpture, tapestries and carpets from the centres of excellence in Europe, especially France and Italy.

He made a remarkable collection of armour, from different periods and different countries. In Milan he bought a job lot of 33 three-quarter suits dating from 1580. Perhaps they had been worn by the private army or bodyguard of one of the Italian princes. About 60 suits of armour are still displayed at Eastnor, though now, to avoid over-statement, they are distributed around the castle. Ruefully he admitted that he did suffer from 'armoritis'.

At Reigate Priory Charles Somers' great achievement was his creation, in the 1850s, of the beautiful neo-classical Library. The building's

exterior can be seen in earlier pictures, but it was the Third Earl who designed its interior, with handsome Ionic pilasters and elegant urns. He furnished it with valuable Indian and Persian carpets, Florentine cabinets, a superb walnut cassone - a chest - inlaid with ivory and with caryatid figures at the corners. Even the titles of the books listed in the library catalogue reflect his highly cultured tastes.

For many months each year the Earl, with Virginia, his beautiful Countess, would leave his estates in the care of his agents, and his children in the care of nurses and governesses.

Visiting Greece and Italy for the sake of his health, he could paint to his heart's content. One of his charming water-colour landscapes was purchased by a local resident at the great Priory Sale in 1921, then most generously donated to our museum by his family sixty years later. So now it is often displayed in the exhibitions mounted in the Earl's elegant library.

The rôle of Reigate Priory has changed, but

Eastnor Castle is still occupied by a member of the Somers family. In 1986 James Hervey-Bathurst inherited the property from his mother who before her marriage was Elizabeth Somers Cocks. The castle, its decorations and furnishings are being beautifully restored, under the guidance of his wife Sarah. Now it is the cherished home of a young family, but open to the public during the summer months and used for corporate entertaining and for advertising. Very successfully, it has appeared in T.V. productions too - as Gatherum Castle in *The Pallisers* and as the setting for *Little Lord Fauntleroy*.

Charles, third Earl Somers, died in 1883. A century after his death, every room in Reigate Priory is used by happy, busy school children, his beautiful library houses a lively museum, the Holbein Hall is often used for public events and the park is used for football, concerts and firework displays. At Eastnor he would be amazed to find coach loads of visitors, camera crews in the drawing room and Land Rovers parked in the forecourt and being demonstrated in the grounds.

Somehow, I think that Isabel Caroline, his spirited eldest daughter, who became Lady Henry Somerset, would take the changes - both at Eastnor and at Reigate Priory - in her stride.

The Library at Reigate Priory showing the blocked arch of the Priory's Great West Door.

This photograph by Francis Frith & Co. shows the south front of the Priory, before Lady Henry Somerset's 1895 alteration. Beyond the bay window was the conservatory. The old pillared main entrance was still in place. The formal sunk garden was newly laid out around a circular pool.

ISABEL SOMERS COCKS
- LADY HENRY SOMERSET

*T*he memory of Lady Isabel Caroline Somers Cocks is still treasured by a few of the older people in and around Reigate, though they remember her by her married name, Lady Henry Somerset. She involved herself in local affairs and in the lives of local people more than any other Priory owner. Her charming, caring personality made her the most deeply loved.

It was in 1971, exactly fifty years after her death, that I became involved with Reigate Priory. And of all the people whose lives I have researched, it is this remarkable lady I would most like to have met, for it is her special personality which seems to have left its impression on the atmosphere of the house.

From her father, the third Earl Somers, Isabel inherited aristocratic social position, property and wealth. She inherited a name which was highly respected and a family tradition of service to the State and to Society. From him too came her artistic talent for painting and sculpture, also her discriminating taste in art, furniture and architecture.

It was from her mother that Isabel inherited charm, vivacity, determination and flair, for Virginia was one of the seven remarkable Pattle sisters, all clever, and all but one, beautiful.

Lady Isabel Somers Cocks 1851-1921

Her father Charles Somers, the artist Earl.

Virginia Pattle - Lady Somers

The Pattle sisters had been brought up mainly in India. Their father, James Pattle, was a wealthy flamboyant Englishman holding a responsible position with the East India Company, but his nickname 'Jim Blazes' reflects his colourful reputation as a heavy drinker and as 'the biggest liar in India'.

Adeline, their mother, was French. She was the daughter of the Chevalier de l'Étang who, around the time of the French Revolution had been a page of Marie Antoinette and then was posted to serve in India at Pondicherry.

The story goes that when James Pattle died in 1845 Adeline carried out his last wishes and with her two youngest daughters proceeded to bring his body back to England, preserved in a cask of spirits. Somehow, perhaps in a storm, the cask split open and on seeing her husband's corpse, poor Adeline died from shock and was buried at sea. Virginia and Sophie continued their voyage, to join their five older sisters who had all married well and settled in England.

So it is not surprising that against this dramatic family background, the Pattle sisters had an intriguing French streak and an air of eastern mystery. Sarah is still remembered as Mrs Toby Prinsep, a leading hostess who gathered around her the leading artists, writers, poets and politicians of the day, and Julia Margaret Cameron - the one who was clever but not beautiful - remains famous as an outstanding pioneer in photography. Descendants of the Pattle sisters include such well known names as Vanessa Bell, Adeline Fisher who married the composer Vaughan Williams, and Virginia Woolf, so all these were related to Isabel Somers.

The most enchanting of all the Pattle sisters was Virginia. She was tall, slim and graceful, and wherever she went, people stopped and gasped in admiration. No wonder that Charles Somers fell in love instantly when he saw G F Watts' picture of her in the Academy Exhibition of 1849. They were married a year later.

Isabel and her sisters

Their first child, Isabel Caroline, was born in 1851, the year of the Great Exhibition. Most of her life was to be spent at Eastnor or at Reigate.

Adeline, a second daughter, was born in 1852 and grew up to marry the Marquess of Tavistock who became 10th Duke of Bedford. We visited Woburn, the Bedford family seat, hoping to find her portrait. To our surprise, we found pictures of Humphrey Parsons and Elizabeth Howard, Countess of Peterborough - but no sign of Adeline, perhaps because her husband died so soon after succeeding to the Dukedom.

At Eastnor, however, and also at Badminton, there are charming paintings by G F Watts showing Isabel and Adeline together as children. Tucked away at Eastnor there is a little chalk drawing of a third daughter, Virginia, who died from diphtheria when she was only four. Isabel remembered her as the naughtiest child who ever lived.

Perhaps it was little Virginia's death, while her parents were on one of their frequent trips abroad, which made the Countess so obsessive about the health of Isabel and Adeline. They were kept away from other children to avoid infection. Strict rules were laid down about their food, clothes, manners and education. Every detail of every waking moment was timetabled and their reading matter was carefully prescribed.

Adeline seems to have been more amenable but Isabel was high-spirited and found the régime intolerable. She adored her beautiful mother, but even as a small child she had a painfully independent mind. Once when she dared to question whether there really was a place called Hell she was locked in her bedroom and fed on bread and water.

Virginia, Third Countess Somers, from a chalk drawing by G. F. Watts.

No wonder that she wore out seven governesses before she was five! There are photographs taken by her aunt, Julia Margaret Cameron, and by that brilliant photographer of children, C L Dodgson (Lewis Carroll), which convey exactly what she felt.

When she was only four Isabel attended a children's party at Buckingham Palace, and when the other children left the ballroom to go to tea, Isabel stayed behind alone, inspecting everything with interest. Queen Victoria came back to look for her, and when she found the small figure sitting on the royal seat she said 'So here is little Isabel'. 'Lady Isabel, if you please', the little girl replied with spirit. Fortunately the Queen **was** amused and, when Isabel was presented at Court many years later, she reminded her of the occasion.

Their mother's letters, carrying instructions and enquiries, show that as the sisters grew up they spent quite a lot of time at Reigate Priory. The large east-facing room above the old Lady Chapel was the night nursery, and their long-suffering nurse would have slept in the small adjoining room.

The pleasant room which faces south over the wooded park was their schoolroom and day-nursery. We can imagine a weary governess, perhaps Miss Severs (not much liked) at her wits' end, or Miss Vickerman, with more success, struggling to keep the attention of the two little girls throughout Monday's timetable. This was German Day, with half hour sessions of German Translation, German Poetry and German Exercise, then Chambers' *Questions,* Grecian History and Music. The French Day, no doubt, was less tiresome, for it reminded the children of the times when they visited their French great-grandmother in Versailles, and there, on a loose rein, they were happy.

If she thought the two little girls seemed off-colour, Countess Somers packed them off to the seaside at Brighton, Cromer, Aberystwyth or Worthing. It was in Brighton, where they attended St Paul's Church, that Isabel began to think seriously about religion. She wrote her own prayers and even made up her mind to become a nun. Somehow, in spite of her mother's vigilance, Isabel secretly read John Stuart Mill's *Essays on Liberty* and was deeply impressed.

As the danger of association with 'male creatures' became apparent, new restrictions were imposed. The Rector of Eastnor had a pupil, Lord Edward Somerset, the fourth son of the Duke of Beaufort, so Isabel and Adeline were warned 'to behave circumspectly and never to be alone with him'.

Lady Isabel Somers

At 19, Isabel left the schoolroom. There were fittings in Paris for her first long dress, to be worn for her first Hunt Ball in the Great Hall at Eastnor Castle. Proudly she walked up and down swishing her long skirt.

Before her presentation at Court she had lessons in curtseying, with rehearsals in that same hall, when Adeline took the part of Queen Victoria and Isabel played her own part of débutante.

Throughout her life, beautiful clothes gave her a special delight. At her coming-out ball, held at their London house, Isabel wore a dress of white tulle, with wreaths and wreaths of jessamine. The tent for the supper was hung with Eastnor tapestry, and the windows of the drawing rooms were taken out, to be replaced by trellises of lilies.

Isabel danced with the Prince, various ambassadors **and** Edward Somerset's older brother, Lord **Henry** Somerset. Numerous parties followed

Lady Isabel at the time of her presentation at Court.

and the name Lord Lorne appears often on her list of partners. To Adeline she wrote: 'I went into dinner with Lorne and had a charming dinner. In the evening he came and sat with Mama and me and was very nice. Next day I sat next Lorne again at dinner and in the evening we sat in the garden.'

At one party, the popular game of 'wishes' was played, and when Isabel's turn came, her wish was to live in the country and have 15 children. Her mother was horrified. 'Of all the horrible indecent things for a young girl to say. What do you suppose they will think of the mother who has brought up such an indelicate daughter?'

But Isabel was very popular and attractive. She had glorious rich chestnut hair and a fresh complexion. She was full of vitality, with the mind of a child to whom everything is new and amazingly interesting.

Isabel came to care deeply for Lord Lorne, and he was at the point of proposing, but Queen Victoria had her own plans for him to marry Princess Louise. Poor Isabel was hurt and bewildered. She rejected all other suitors, including Lord Henry Somerset.

Isabel even considered becoming a Sister of Mercy - but, as an heiress, it was her **duty** to marry. She could at least marry a good man and have a large family.

Soon, Lord Henry Somerset came to Eastnor and proposed again.

Unfortunately, Isabel's mother persuaded her to accept, for Lord Henry, though only a second son, was after all the son of the Duke of Beaufort, the ancient family of the Plantagenets. He moved in Court circles, he was a Privy Counsellor, an M P and a J P.

They were married at St George's, Hanover Square, in February 1872. Her six bridesmaids were dressed in white silk, with white tippets and sky blue silk hats. Isabel carried a basket of snowdrops, gathered for her that morning by Lord Tennyson.

Lady Henry Somerset

From this time Isabel was known always as Lady Henry Somerset, adding only two letters to her maiden name to make her married surname.

Isabel's married life was centred at Badminton, the Beaufort family seat in Gloucestershire. Though this was an ancient and impressive stately home, life there was free and uninhibited. The only restriction was that indoors she must always wear

Badminton House, Gloucestershire, the country seat of the Somersets, Dukes of Beaufort.

white kid gloves! The Duke and Duchess loved her and fondly called her 'Quaily', for she was short and a little plump. At Eastnor there is a delightful portrait of Isabel at this time, painted, not surprisingly, by G F Watts. On Isabel's wrist Watts painted a little brown bird - a quail! Watts must have painted a copy of this picture, for he gave one to Isabel for herself. Isabel passed this on to the daughter of one of her gardeners, who treasured it, though it was rather badly damaged. Half a century later, when she showed it to her grandson who was at school at the Priory, he proudly brought it for us to see, and a skilled photographer parent produced a perfect print. This is shown in our colour section.

At first, Isabel was very happy at Badminton. She had her own horse and carriage, and could go where she liked, when she liked. Her vitality, gaiety and laughter endeared her to her tall brothers-in-law, and the young people had fun. 'She is the sunshine of our house', said the Duke.

Her son, Henry Somers Somerset, was born after two years, but the marriage was not a success. When Isabel discovered her husband embracing a young footman she was horrified. Victorian ladies were expected to turn a blind eye to their husbands' shortcomings but, following her mother's advice, Isabel left Badminton and fled with her little son back to her parents' home at Eastnor.

She had put herself in the wrong, both socially and legally, and Victorian society reacted unkindly. The charming love-songs composed by Lord Henry Somerset were sung in respectable drawing-rooms throughout the land, so surely Lady Henry

Somerset must be evil-minded. She had 'invented a dreadful new sin and spoken of something only mentioned in the Bible'. For years, many homes were closed to her, gentlemen did not acknowledge her, even her sister had to see her privately and ladies drew their skirts away as she passed.

To be treated as an outcast was devastating, but it was this experience which deepened Isabel's compassion for others in the future.

Legally, a father had rights over his son, especially in such a great family as the Beauforts, where succession was involved. The long and painful process of litigation was another ordeal to endure. Isabel brought her little son to Reigate Priory and waited quietly. Much later she wrote in her diary 'Thirty years ago the Law gave me my child. The lilacs were in bloom in the Priory garden and I watched and waited till the telegram came, then I fell on my knees to thank God.'

The *Monthly Illustrated Journal*, June 1878, reported 'The Law Courts have decided that Lady Henry Somerset, and not the husband, from whom she is separated, is to retain possession of the little boy, now four years old. Mr Justice Field, who investigated the case, declared that Lady Henry Somerset is a lady whose conduct is irreproachable.'

So the young Henry was brought up mainly by his mother and was educated by tutors at home, though he did spend some time with his father's parents, the Beauforts, at Badminton. Later he went to Marlborough and on to Balliol College, Oxford.

His father, Lord Henry Somerset remained a Privy Counsellor till his death, but withdrew from his responsibilities as M P for Monmouthshire and as Controller of Queen Victoria's Household. He left the country and settled in Florence where he died in 1932.

Isabel at the Priory

Isabel decided to settle at the Priory. She threw herself into managing her father's Reigate estate, trying hard to understand all the wrangles over sand, gravel, commons and trees. She cared for her father's tenants and took an active part in local affairs.

But inwardly, she was desolate and wrestled with doubts about God. One day, she sat thinking in her favourite retreat, her tree house by the Priory lake. 'Is there really a Supreme Being?' was the burning question. Suddenly the answer came 'Act as if I were, and you will know that I am'.

Now Isabel prayed and read her Bible

The figure of a child, made by Lady Henry, which stood on the altar of her private chapel at Reigate Priory.

conscientiously. In the north west corner of the Priory she made herself a tiny private chapel. Under the tuition of her friends the artist G F Watts and his wife Mary, she lovingly made the furnishings herself - a window of stained glass, a sculpted figure of a child with outstretched arms, and an embroidered altar-cloth. The window and the altar figure survive in the Museum's care, but the room now has a different use - for a cloakroom and toilets!

Fortunately, Isabel was resilient. She was still only 27, she delighted in parties, beautiful clothes and beautiful surroundings. She began to entertain and she made new friends. Gradually Isabel began to find herself accepted again and was even invited to Drawing Rooms and a State Ball at Buckingham Palace.

An old *Surrey Mirror* contained a detailed report of a Fancy Dress Ball held at the Priory on January 13th 1883. Almost 200 people came - relations, titled friends, leading local personalities. The report gives the menu, in French of course, the programme of music, mainly Strauss and Sullivan, and the costume worn by each guest - Mary Queen of Scots, Sir Walter Raleigh, Night, Rouge et Noir, a Grape

Gatherer and so on. Isabel herself is described as wearing a costume 'temps Louis XVI, a white and pink dress trimmed with panel embroidery and powdered hair surmounted by a tiara of pearls'. The reporter remarked 'It seems almost a pity that some of the guests did not think to more closely connect the past with the present. We might thus have been introduced to William de Warenne, the Countess of Peterborough, Sir John Parsons or Lord Monson.' (In 1985, just over a century later, we did just that!)

For some years, Isabel gave a home to her two young cousins, Laura Gurney and Blanche Clogstoun. On June 26th 1883, when Blanche was married to Herbert Somers Cocks, the ceremony at the parish church was followed by a glittering reception at the Priory. The marriage certificate was hardly large enough for the names of the witnesses Virginia Somers, Lord Tavistock (Adeline's husband), G F Watts, Isabelle (sic) Somerset and many more. A Triumphal Arch spanned the Priory entrance in Bell Street, decorations adorned the railway station and most of the streets in Reigate were decorated.

Isabel devoted a lot of her time and energy to the welfare of the tenants and to the poor and needy in Reigate. Laura Gurney, who was only 13, wrote: 'She simply radiated charm, it seemed to shine from her like an atmosphere. Her sympathy was much more than a general wish to help people. She projected herself into the whole question of the trouble and showed a vivid burning interest betrayed in countless quick questions, after which she would think it over in silence for a moment, then there would be definite action. If people were hungry they must be fed, at once, from her own kitchen. If they were cold, clothes were dispatched and blankets taken from the Priory beds, then and there. The whole trend of her mind was democratic and there was no stuffiness or barrier of any kind with those in other classes.'

Great responsibilities

Charles, third Earl Somers, died in September 1883, so Isabel inherited not only Reigate Priory with all its manorial properties, but also Eastnor Castle with its own vast estates and valuable land in London, known as Somers Town. Lady Henry Somerset, as we ought to call her, now became a very wealthy woman with great responsibilities. At first she moved to Eastnor and devoted herself seriously to

An alley in Ledbury, restored from its nineteenth-century squalor.

her duties there as a landowner, and also, as in Reigate, to caring for her tenants.

Three miles from Eastnor is Ledbury. Now it is a charming little town with beautifully restored black and white buildings, but in the nineteenth century it was rather different. The tannery, breweries, sewage in the open drains, animals and human beings made it a place of smells, filth and poverty. It was notorious for the depravity which flourished there.

Somehow, Lady Henry met a group of Methodists. The most shining example among them was a Mrs Ridley, who took Isabel into the squalid streets to see how the poorest people lived. Soon Isabel was deeply involved caring for these people and she even established a Mission Hall in the grimiest street of all - Bye Street. We found it now used as a chapel. She realised that drunkenness was at the root of much of the misery she had seen and she set to work to do all she could to cure this evil.

People of her own class thought she was a traitor - but she was beginning to find her purpose in life. She believed in temperance, but realised that only a firm example would be effective, so she signed the

Total Abstinence pledge and arranged for all her employees to sign too. All the contents of the wine-cellars at Reigate Priory and at Eastnor Castle had to be poured down the drains!

We see how human she was, when we hear how, on her way to sign the pledge along with all her servants at Eastnor, she went to the refreshment room on Worcester station and drank, with great relish, two glasses of fruity port, knowing they would be her last.

Lady Henry threw herself fervently into work for the temperance cause, and by 1890, she was President of the British Women's Temperance Association.

She was charming, she was persuasive, she was forceful, she was titled. She made a great impact and was soon addressing meetings all over the country. Next she was invited to make a lecture tour in America, where she enthralled audiences of thousands. It was at this time that she met Florence Willard - her American counterpart - and they were to become close friends.

When Lady Henry returned to England she found that the executive committee of the BWTA had become highly critical of their President - she had 'too wide an outlook, too vast an energy, too progressive a mind'. They were insisting on **Total** Abstinence, while Lady Henry had a wider perspective. She was even expressing her views on such unmentionables as Women's Suffrage, the Opium Problem and the protection of women from venereal disease.

A ballot was taken and Lady Henry Somerset won through, for her views were shared by the more realistic middle class women who formed the main body of the membership. Women all over the country wore a bow of white ribbon (later a brooch) as a sign of their support for the temperance cause. Years of hard work followed. She had to have a staff of secretaries and stenographers wherever she went.

The Priory Grounds

Isabel must have had unbounded energy, for simultaneously she was working on two great projects. Over these years she was carrying out extensive improvements at Reigate Priory. She loved the building and understood its history. She treasured the works of art already there - the Holbein fireplace, the Verrio wall paintings and the superb staircase. Early in her married life she

The windows of the Grand Priory staircase, fitted with stained glass showing the arms of the Somers and Somerset families.

The Eagle Gateway was moved to the courtyard in 1893. The canopy over the new main entrance can just be seen on the left.

replaced some of the staircase windows with stained glass depicting the coats of arms of both families - the Somers and the Somersets.

She turned her attention too to the Priory's fine Eagle Gateway in Bell Street. Unfortunately this was straight opposite the Castle public house! This was most inappropriate - so the whole entrance was moved to its present position on the west side of the courtyard, so that her coachman and visitors would not be corrupted by passing so many public houses. The Eagle pillars and the wrought iron screens are now listed, in their own right, separately from the Priory building. In 1993 the eagles were splendidly restored by English

Another Frith photograph, taken from the Eagle Gateway just before it was moved in 1893.

Heritage. The screens, we hope, will come next.

Work was started to create a sunk garden on the south front. As the gardeners dug to lower the level they began to uncover human bones. Almost certainly this area had been the old garth and these were the bones of Augustinian canons. Lady Henry decided to leave them undisturbed and to create the sunk garden further south beyond the ancient foundations of the south cloister buildings.

Photographs show how the gardens progressed, with clipped yew and holly bushes, arbours and archways, yet still leaving a clear view of the park and the wooded hill to the south. In 1917, an American family who were renting the Priory gained Lady Henry's permission to plant an Irish yew hedge enclosing this beautiful garden. But she expressed her wish that in the centres of the hedges of the east and west sides, the yews should be cut in the form of crosses, as a reminder that this is still consecrated ground. These crosses were maintained until the 1970s when over-zealous gardeners destroyed them in seconds with their mechanical hedge trimmers. It would be rather nice to grow back the crosses, for the garden is still used as a peaceful retreat.

Following her father's example, Lady Henry had specimen trees planted around the park. The herbaceous borders beside the 'Monk's Walk' on the west side were especially splendid. She made 'tennis lawns' near the house, also a rose garden and lily pond. Towards the lake a nine-hole golf course was constructed, and the old bowls lawn to the east of the house was laid out for croquet. In the boat house by the four-acre lake a 14' punt was kept.

Her interest in golf was not limited to the Priory. One of her contributions to Reigate life was the establishment of the Reigate Heath Golf Club. As Lord of the Manor she made a large area available for the course, and she became the first President of the Club which was founded in 1895. She opened the course for play in April 1896 and provided the Clubhouse which she opened the following year.

For centuries the Priory's kitchen gardens had supplied the fruit and vegetables for the household. Until recently the whitewashed walls of the greenhouses, the peach house, vine house, 'small span' house and the cucumber house could still be seen. The Priory accounts show us that surplus produce was often sold to the townspeople. Now we have a supermarket on that site instead!

The families of some of those faithful gardeners still live in Reigate - there were Mr Wickens, Arthur Barrett, Henry Turner, James Jordan, James Matthews - and Mr Coomber, gardener here for fifty years.

The Priory Building

High on the east wall of the Eagle Courtyard there is a carved inscription in Latin, commemorating the vast alterations and extensions which were

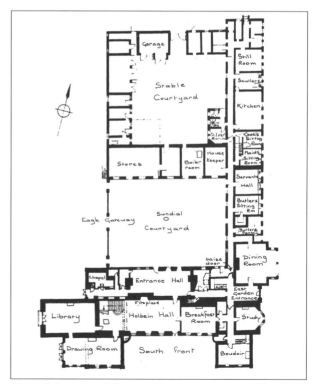

Plan of the ground floor, as the rooms were used in 1919.

Replica of the seal of William de Warenne (obverse). The shield and the richly emblazoned trappings are decorated with the chequy Warenne design.
Photograph by Mike Couchman.

The Priory seal – a replica made in green wax. The original seals were usually red and about 4 cm in diameter. The shield and the W monogram on the reverse refer to the Warenne founder. Finding part of an authentic example in Cambridge was an important recent discovery.
Photograph by Mike Couchman.

This portrait, painted on wood, is labelled John Lymden, the last Prior of Reigate.
It is typically Tudor and full of clues. The rings, the palm leaf and the cap badges each have a significance.
One shield was overpainted in the Victorian era with the badge of Knights Hospitallers
and this was adopted as the Priory School badge in 1948.
Photograph by Mike Couchman.

The gleaming stone fireplace, showing the shield of William Howard, symbolises the transition from the austerity of the Priory Church to the warmth and grandeur of an important family's home. The magnificent carved oak overmantel was commissioned by Henry VIII and probably designed by H ans Hoblein. It was installed at Bletchingley Place, possibly for the divorced Queen, Anne of Cleves, and moved to Reigate by 1655.

Photograph by Mike Couchman.

*Lord Charles Howard, Queen Elizabeth's Lord High Admiral. Portrayed in 1988
by Vera and Ray Strank for the exhibition at Reigate Priory – his favourite home – to celebrate the
400th anniversary of his victory over the Spanish Armada.*

*Elizabeth Howard, Countess of Peterborough – Charles Howard's grand-daughter – was
one of the celebrated seventeenth-century beauties painted by Sir Anthony Van Dyck.
This original portrait is at Wilton House, but copies can be seen
in stately homes throughout the country.*

*Jupiter and Juno, Vulcan and Venus, Hercules and Hymen – all these and many more
gods and goddesses adorn the ceiling and the walls of the Priory's Grand Staircase.
Surrey County Council has a programme of much-needed restoration.*

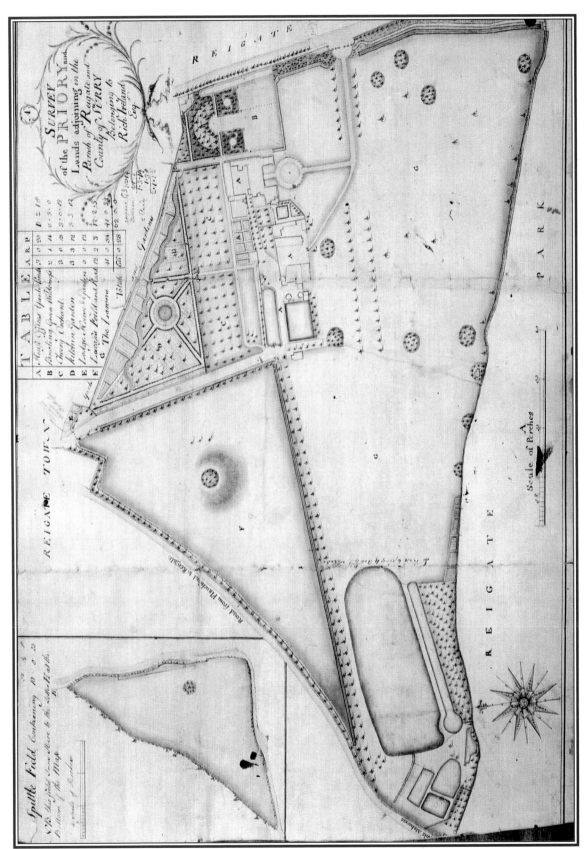

Discovered in an attic, this survey shows the Priory lands belonging to Richard Ireland around 1770.
It is precise and remarkably informative.
Photograph by Malcolm Pendrill

A splendid menu on vellum, rolled and tied with scarlet ribbons, with calligraphy by Anthony Wood, awaited each guest at the Banquet held in the Holbein Hall in 1985 to celebrate the founding of Reigate Priory. The Duke of Norfolk attended as Guest of Honour, and every visitor appeared in costume representing a character in the Priory's life. Each course on the menu related to some period in the Priory's story. Banners decorated the ancient walls, a jester and singers provided lively entertainment.

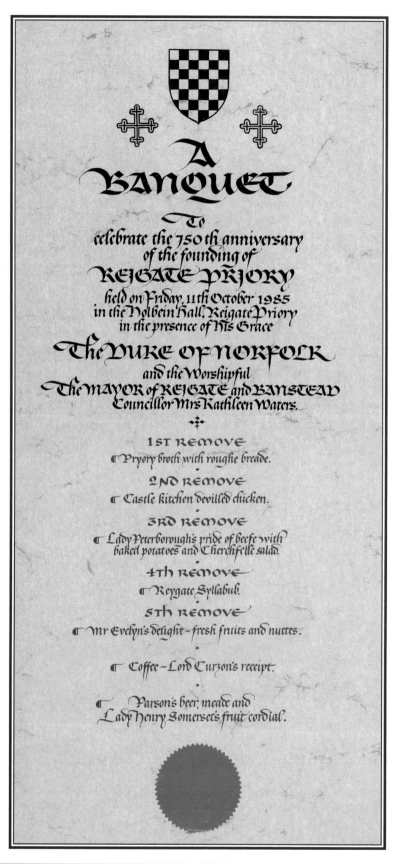

A
BANQUET
To celebrate the 750th anniversary of the founding of
REIGATE PRIORY
held on Friday, 11th October 1985 in the Holbein Hall, Reigate Priory in the presence of His Grace
The DUKE OF NORFOLK
and the Worshipful
The MAYOR of REIGATE and BANSTEAD Councillor Mrs Kathleen Waters.

1ST REMOVE
Pryory broth with roughe breade.

2ND REMOVE
Castle kitchen devilled chicken.

3RD REMOVE
Lady Peterborough's pride of beefe with baked potatoes and Cherchfelle salad.

4TH REMOVE
Reygate Syllabub.

5TH REMOVE
Mr Evelyn's delight – fresh fruits and nuttes.

Coffee – Lord Curzon's receipt.

Parson's beer, meade and Lady Henry Somerset's fruit cordial.

Two pictures painted by the Somers' family friend, G F Watts.
Top: Isabel and Adeline, aged about eight and seven – shown here by kind permission of the
Duke of Beaufort.Bottom: Isabel, nick-named 'Quaily', around the time of her marriage to
Lord Henry Somerset, second son of the eighth Duke of Beaufort.

A photograph recently discovered in a local family album, showing Lady Henry Somerset in the Priory Drawing Room in the 1880s. The curtained window in the background was in the southern of the two bays designed by Searles for the west end of the building. On the table is a photograph o f her father, the third Earl Somers, and above is the painting which we found at Badminton, showing her little son Henry.

The Priory Drawing Room, extended in 1895 to twice its former length. This photograph, taken from the west end, shows the firescreen, ornaments and pictures used again to furnish the room. The catalogue from the Sale of Contents in 1921 lists many of these in fascinating detail.

The Holbein Hall, photographed by Frith in the 1890s. At that time the walls were panelled, the Wolsey ceiling was plastered in a design copied from Hampton Court and Sir John Parson's magnificent chandelier was still in place. The long-case clock on the half-landing was regularly wound by a local clock maker.

Reigate Priory School aims to provide the best possible education in a lively, caring and stimulating atmosphere.
Pictures from the school prospectus show a wide range of activities.
Photographs by Patrick Connolly.

The Market Place and the history of shopping was the theme for the Priory Museum's exhibition in 1996. This large mural, designed and painted by Barbara Ferguson, is full of detail. It shows a medieval market – Reigate perhaps – where a Black Canon can be seen mingling with the townsfolk and the miller (strangely like the 20th Century Priory caretaker, Don Holman) leans from an upstairs window.

On facing page: Some of the people behind the scenes who create the colourful, exciting and interactive exhibitions at the Priory.

Past, present and FUTURE.
Photograph by Patrick Connolly

Lady Henry Somerset's new dining room.

made to the Priory building between 1893 and 1895. For this great enterprise Lady Henry employed John Pollen, a highly cultivated and religious man who, like the third Earl Somers, was an accomplished artist.

These improvements to the Priory cost nearly £20,000. A new entrance was created from the inner courtyard, with a large entrance hall made from three smaller rooms. Two carved oak Jacobean chimney pieces were brought from Castleditch, the

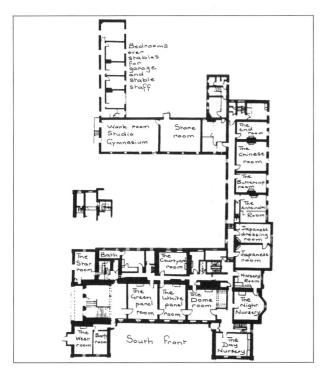

Plan of the first floor, with rooms named as they were in 1919.

Somers' dismantled manor house, and placed one at each end.

Recently a local collector discovered, in the album of a well-known local family, a photograph showing Lady Henry relaxing in her small drawing room in the south west wing, some time in the 1880s. In 1895 the conservatory, shown in earlier pictures of the Priory, and also the west-facing bay window designed by Searles, were taken down so that the drawing room could be greatly extended. We have a later Victorian photograph of this room. Many of the pictures and pieces of furniture are the same in the two photographs, some are listed in the 1921 Priory sale book, and some we have come across again in our visits to Eastnor and Badminton.

The east side of the building, north of the old Lady Chapel, was replaced by a much longer range of buildings, to provide a splendid new dining room, light and airy kitchens, and servants' quarters. On the first floor above were spacious bedrooms for family and guests and above those were pleasant attic rooms for servants. Lady Henry was deeply concerned for the welfare of all her employees.

The new dining room was, and still is, impressive, with a large square bay window. The plasterwork ceiling is especially beautiful and is designed around Lady Henry's initials I (for Isabel), C (for Caroline), S C (for Somers Cocks) and S (for Somerset). The doors and the furniture were beautifully carved, and on the corner dressers were fine Venetian pharmacy jars. In the centre hung an exquisite Venetian glass chandelier. The walls were lined with silk damask and the curtains were panels of old Italian embroidery. Two antique Indian carpets covered the dark oak floor. Photographs survive, showing the room in her day, but we have to imagine the rich red colour scheme.

Above, the new bedrooms were furnished and decorated, each to a theme. Over the dining room there was the Japanese Bedroom with its Dressing Room, then the Antoinette Bedroom, the Buttercup Bedroom and the Chinese Bedroom.

A second courtyard, paved, with a central drain, gave extra stabling for twelve horses. There were coachmen's quarters and more rooms for outside staff. There was a garage for three large cars, and in the corner, a Cycle Shed!

Lady Henry had taken to cycling - on a tricycle. She even became President of the Mowbray House Cycling Association, to encourage women to assert their independence and to improve their health by

Lady Henry Somerset on her tricycle.

The streets of Reigate were eleborately decorated to welcome the newly-married Henry and Katherine Somerset.

taking to the wheel. This was a co-operative enterprise, helping members to buy shares in bicycles. They had their own club colours - light blue, dark blue and white. Sometimes marquees were erected on the Priory lawns, for the rallies and picnics which Lady Henry organised.

Not only did she cycle around the Priory grounds accompanied by her friends and the family pets, but she went off with Miss Willard and another friend on a cycling tour through France. In the event, they abandoned their holiday to organise relief work for a party of Armenian refugees who had been landed at Marseilles.

Henry Somers Somerset

The Priory alterations and extensions were completed in time to celebrate the 21st birthday of the young Henry Somerset. In July 1895 three hundred guests were entertained to supper at the Priory. The grounds were illuminated and a band

played on the lawn. The following year there were more celebrations when Henry was married to Lady Katherine de Vere Beauclerk, daughter of the Duke and Duchess of St Albans. (Now, with Somerset, Beaufort and St Albans, we have our full score of Somers-related street names.) After the ceremony and reception in London, the bride and bridegroom travelled to Reigate by special train and their carriage was pulled to the Priory by estate employees.

An original programme, which was given to our Museum many years ago by Mr Walter Bushby, gives a vivid picture of another interesting event. This was held on Saturday December 1st 1906 at 3 p.m. and 8 p.m..

'A dramatised Version of

Bunyan's

PILGRIM'S PROGRESS

will be performed at

Reigate Priory
(by kind permission of Lady Katherine Somerset)'

Patrons included the Duchess of St Albans (Lady Katherine's mother), Adeline, Duchess of Bedford, and Lady Henry Somerset. The music was arranged by Mr R Vaughan Williams, who conducted the orchestra (and choir - added in pencil). Vaughan Williams' wife was Adeline Fisher, Lady Henry's

Makepeace, Lady Henry's Dower House, was built in Park Lane on the site of Reigate's old workhouse.

The reredos at St Luke's Church, South Park, was painted by Lady Henry 'in a time of much bodily pain and weakness'. The gilded candlesticks were given in 1906 by Lady Katherine Somerset, Lady Henry's daughter-in-law.

cousin, once removed. They lived only five miles away, at Dorking.

This event was in aid of the Guild of the Brave Poor Things, which developed into the Chailey Heritage for blind and crippled folk.

The parts of Faith, Hope and Charity were taken by Ruth, Rachel and Ursula Charrington, daughters, by a first marriage, of Mrs Hadley of Parkside, South Park. A very old lady who had been one of the little girls taking part as an angel, told how Lady Henry made them rest between performances on the magnificent canopied beds in the state bedrooms above the Holbein Hall.

We know that Lady Katherine and Lady Henry, when she was in Reigate, were regular worshippers and generous supporters of St Luke's Church in South Park. Sometimes with visitors and members

of the household they walked across the park to St Luke's, where there was a private Priory pew in the south aisle. Lady Henry created the unusual reredos herself. The two huge gilded candlesticks and the old Italian carved and gilded crucifix, which were donated by Lady Katherine, are still in use.

Soon after her son's marriage Lady Henry had conveyed to him all her Reigate properties, including the Priory. She continued to play a part in local affairs and built Makepeace, near the Park Lane entrance, as her dower house. Sometimes she still used her London flat, but much of her time was now spent at Duxhurst, the village of her own creation.

In 1900 Lady Henry passed over her Eastnor estate to her cousin Arthur, who had inherited the barony, but not the earldom, on her father's death. He subsequently became Chief Scout and was the grandfather of the present owner.

The Duxhurst Homes

Over these years Lady Henry was devoting more and more time to the welfare of women. For some years she ran a newspaper *The Women's Signal*, but her greatest achievement by far was the establishment of a home for alcoholic women.

Her work for temperance had taken her all over the country, but in London's East End she saw the most tragic cases of alcoholism, leading to untold misery. Lady Henry cared especially for women and children whose lives were broken and hopeless, and so had the inspiration to create a village settlement, where they could be given a new chance

Duxhurst, where alcoholic women and needy children were restored to health.

of a healthy, happy life. She bought a manor house and farm at Duxhurst, three miles south of the Priory, just beyond Sidlow Bridge. This description appeared in *Whitaker's Almanack*:

'The Industrial Farm Colony at Duxhurst, Reigate, for the reception of Inebriate Women, was founded in 1894 by Lady Henry Somerset.

'The plan on which this Colony is worked is that of a model village standing among the Surrey hills on a farm of 180 acres. The village consists of home-like cottages grouped round an open quadrangle with a small church adjacent, and at a short distance, the Superintendent's cottage and the Chaplain's lodge. In each cottage about ten or twelve patients are received, and are presided over by a Cottage Sister.

'Attached to the village also are a dining hall, kitchens, a recreation hall, laundries, workshops and workrooms, together with a hospital into which every patient is received on first arrival in the Colony.

'The patients are engaged in outdoor work in the gardens and on the farm, and are taught weaving, embroidery, basket making, and domestic employments.

'The life on the Farm Colony is for children as well as women. Thirty-two are received in a separate home. Their presence is essential to a normal domestic life, and it brings joy and brightness as nothing else can. They are often the best and most inspiring object-lesson the women

can look upon. Many of them are sent by the National Society for the Prevention of Cruelty to Children, and are brought up in the Colony. Some of the mothers also who are in the Colony for a longer period under sentence of the Inebriate Acts (1879) have been allowed to bring their children, and these are cared for in the Children's Home.

'A weekly payment is charged for all patients, but in most cases this does not cover the expense, which has to be supplemented by contributions from outside sources.'

Though Lady Henry poured in all her own resources, the financing of this great enterprise was always a problem. She even mortgaged the Priory and sold Somers Town, the valuable property in London.

At Duxhurst Isabel worked tirelessly as Superintendent, even dressing and working as a nurse herself. Her home there, The Cottage, remains today.

There are still a few people with vivid memories of 'My Lady' - one of them is Lilian Brown of Charlwood, now over ninety years old. When her mother died, Lilian, a little girl of seven, was rescued by Lady Henry Somerset from London's East End, given a new life at Duxhurst, then trained as a maid at The Cottage. Lilian Brown has written down her memories, under the title *Rags to Riches*, and she describes hot summer days when the children walked from Duxhurst across the fields and up into the Priory park carrying hampers of

Lady Henry at the door of The Cottage, her home at Duxhurst.

The little wooden figure of St Rita.

food for their annual picnic. Though it was a long way for the little ones, who had to be carried 'piggy back' or on crossed hands, it was worth it, to see the lake, the ducks, the swans, the beautiful gardens and the Priory house which to them was a palace.

Lady Henry had remarkable gifts of compassion and understanding. As well as providing medical care, she restored the self-respect of her patients, often starting with a visit to the Reigate shops to buy a new pair of stays, a new dress or a new hat. The services in the little church, so beautiful inside, along with the atmosphere of peace and of patient love, restored their confidence. The practical activities, the crafts and the gardening gave the women a sense of achievement and the domestic work gave them a new pattern for home-making.

In the Manor House, at the west end of the village, there were the 'ladies' too, for she took in patients from every social level. One of these was Ethel de Neve, mistress of the notorious Dr Crippen. There were titled ladies, famous opera singers and others who could pay a little more and

were used to a different pattern of life. All Lady Henry's patients arrived broken and hopeless, and though some were incurable, a success rate of over 73 per cent was achieved.

On the mantelpiece in 'The Cottage' was one of Lady Henry's most cherished possessions, a little carved wooden figure of a nun, painted and gilded. It was dancing and happy, and appropriately represented St Rita, the Saint of the Impossibles.

Lady Henry's own artistic ability had many outlets. She had a talent for sculpture and pottery. At some time she visited the Potters' Art Guild works at Compton, founded by Mary Watts, the second wife of the artist G F Watts. When she found that there was suitable clay at Duxhurst she installed a kiln and employed experienced potters as teachers for her patients. The excellent pottery they produced there - in simple shapes and beautiful clear luminous greens, blues and yellows, was sold mainly at Selfridge's and is now avidly collected.

On the end wall of the Priory's east wing there is an enigmatic memorial. The local Heritage Trust placed a sundial there, showing the trademark for the pottery, a boy on a duck's back (for Duxhurst). The explanation, a written memorial to Lady Henry Somerset, is in the hallway of the building.

Like her father, Lady Henry painted many beautiful pictures. There is a delightful book of poems for children which she wrote and illustrated at Reigate Priory. *Our Village Life* was published in 1884 and sold 'to support a home recently opened for workhouse girls. At an early age they are taken from our City Unions and trained for laundry and household work.' Perhaps this was produced especially to support the home she had opened in Upper West Street, Reigate, now a private house. Copies of this charming book are now - like the pottery - collectors' pieces.

From newspapers, national and local, it is evident that Lady Henry was spending all her time and energy, not only on caring for her patients and maintaining the work of the village at Duxhurst, but she was speaking and appearing at countless

Tribute to Lady Henry Somerset, Temple Gardens, London.

meetings, laying foundation stones, opening many local buildings, writing letters and supporting hosts of good causes. Her health was giving cause for concern, but she took no notice.

Lady Henry died at her London flat, almost 70 years old, on March 10th 1921, after an operation for appendicitis and only two days' illness. Her funeral service was held at St Alban's, Holborn, and she was buried at the Brookwood Cemetery near Woking. Though she is not buried with her parents at Eastnor, we found several memorials to her, the drinking fountain on the village green and the terrace behind the castle overlooking the lake.

In London we found a charming tribute, recently restored, in the Temple Gardens. It is the figure of a child, holding a bowl, with the inscription:

'From children of the Loyal Temperance Legion, in memory of work done for the temperance cause by Lady Henry Somerset, President of the National British Women's Temperance Association, Incorporated.

"I was thirsty and ye gave me drink"' (Water, of course!). In Portland, Maine, there is a replica, set up by her American admirers.

Without Lady Henry the colony at Duxhurst lost its driving force, and eventually the land was put up for sale. The cottages have gone, and the chapel, but recently the font was restored and installed at Emmanuel Church, Sidlow Bridge, with an inscription which ends:

'The Spirit of the Lord God is upon me
To give unto them beauty for ashes (Isa. 61).'

Beauty for Ashes was the title of her own book about Duxhurst. But her true memorial lives on in the transformed lives of the thousands of women and children she loved and cared for.

The Great Sale of Reigate

Lady Henry's death marked the end of an era. Her family had owned Reigate Priory for well over a century, and the Manor of Reigate for twice as long. She had been generous and caring to all her tenants and a leading figure both locally and nationally.

Her son's marriage to Katherine Beauclerk had been happy for some years, while their sons Henry, John and Edward were growing up. A memento from that time remains just inside the Bell Street car park, where we can see the row of little gravestones where their pet dogs were buried.

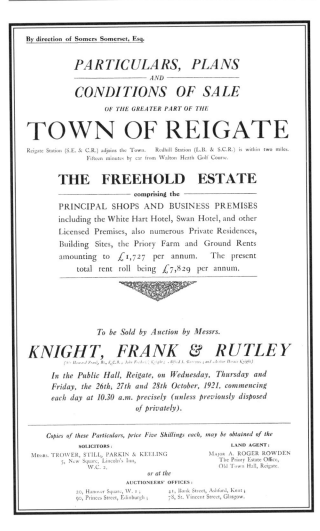

By direction of Somers Somerset, Esq.

PARTICULARS, PLANS

— AND —

CONDITIONS OF SALE

OF THE GREATER PART OF THE

TOWN OF REIGATE

Reigate Station (S.E. & C.R.) adjoins the Town.   Redhill Station (L.B. & S.C.R.) is within two miles.
Fifteen minutes by car from Walton Heath Golf Course.

THE FREEHOLD ESTATE

— comprising the —

PRINCIPAL SHOPS AND BUSINESS PREMISES
including the White Hart Hotel, Swan Hotel, and other
Licensed Premises, also numerous Private Residences,
Building Sites, the Priory Farm and Ground Rents
amounting to £1,727 per annum.   The present
total rent roll being £7,829 per annum.

To be Sold by Auction by Messrs.

KNIGHT, FRANK & RUTLEY

(Sir Howard Frank, Bt., K.C.B., John Frederick Knight ; Alfred L. Burrows ; and Arthur Howe Knight)

In the Public Hall, Reigate, on Wednesday, Thursday and
Friday, the 26th, 27th and 28th October, 1921, commencing
each day at 10.30 a.m. precisely (unless previously disposed
of privately).

Copies of these Particulars, price Five Shillings each, may be obtained of the

SOLICITORS :	LAND AGENT :
Messrs. TROWER, STILL, PARKIN & KEELING	Major A. ROGER ROWDEN
5, New Square, Lincoln's Inn,	The Priory Estate Office,
W.C. 2.	Old Town Hall, Reigate.

or at the

AUCTIONEERS' OFFICES :

20, Hanover Square, W. 1 ;   41, Bank Street, Ashford, Kent ;
90, Princes Street, Edinburgh ;   78, St. Vincent Street, Glasgow.

We had heard little about Henry Somers Somerset, but not long ago the Museum received a scrap book of newspaper cuttings recording his unsuccessful campaign when he stood as a Liberal candidate for Croydon in 1906. His grandson, the present Duke of Beaufort, immediately recognised his grandmother's handwriting when we showed the album to him. Henry Somers Somerset loved travelling, riding, hunting and he was an adventurous balloonist, attached for a while to the French army. He served with distinction in the Boer and 1914-18 wars and was awarded the OBE.

Sadly, his marriage failed and in 1919, with his mother's full agreement, he offered the Priory for sale, but no offers were made. In February 1920 a public-spirited local corn-merchant, Mr Randal Vogan, paid £15,000 for Reigate Park, to the south of the Priory Lands, and he and his wife presented this beautiful wooded area to the people of Reigate 'for their quiet enjoyment'. A stone memorial seat on the ridge - and two street names, Randal Crescent and Vogan Close - record their generosity.

There was an offer from a wealthy financier to buy the whole of the Somers' Reigate estate, but Henry Somers Somerset and Lady Henry were anxious that all tenants should have a chance to buy their own freehold. They were even to be allowed to leave two thirds of the purchase price on mortgage.

In August 1921, following Lady Henry Somerset's death, the Great Sale of Reigate was held in the Public Hall on the High Street. The town properties, businesses and homes, the White Hart and Swan hotels, even the Old Town Hall, were sold to hundreds of mainly local buyers. The Town Hall went to Randal Vogan, who presented it as his second gift to the town in 1922. Many of the old catalogues, carefully annotated with the prices the properties fetched, are still greatly prized by local families.

In September the Priory itself was purchased by Admiral and Countess Beatty, and the contents were sold separately later. The beautifully illustrated catalogue is particularly fascinating and informative for us today, and we have come across some of the pictures and pieces of furniture at Eastnor, at Badminton and in homes in Reigate.

The Great Sale of Reigate was one of the most moving events in the town's history.

When Henry Somers Somerset passed all the remaining manorial rights to the Borough, both the Somers link and the medieval system of land ownership came to an end.

It is interesting that, because the tenth Duke of Beaufort had no direct heir when he died in 1982, it was Lady Henry Somerset's great-grandson David who became the eleventh Duke and is now head of the great Plantagenet family - the Beauforts at Badminton. At both Eastnor and Badminton the family connections with Reigate Priory and their memories of Lady Henry Somerset are still greatly valued.

Pictures of their Priory tenancy treasured by the Jaffray family for over a century.

TENANTS AND VISITORS

he windows of the Priory building are still fitted with sturdy wooden shutters and flat, heavy iron bars which swing over and latch firmly into sockets to keep them closed. Today these are very useful for security and for black-out, when television, films or slides are in use.

When the house was in private ownership the windows were often shuttered for months at a time. The main rooms would be eerily dark and the furniture shrouded in dust sheets.

Like so many wealthy landowners, then as now, the Somers family lived for only part of the year in each of their properties. They spent quite long periods visiting friends or relations, and even longer periods travelling abroad. Ladies' maids, valets and other personal staff would have accompanied the family, but the house and estate staff remained to maintain the establishment and to tackle repairs, refurbishments and the annual cleaning.

Sometimes, if the owners were not in residence, the housekeeper would be called upon to give conducted tours of the building to 'gentlefolk' who were exploring the district. Such events are elegantly described in Jane Austen's novels.

There is a story of an occasion when Lady Henry Somerset and a friend disguised themselves and acted as visitors to Eastnor Castle. When they collapsed with laughter halfway through the tour, the poor housekeeper was quite distraught. Lady Henry had a delightful sense of fun and a bubbling laugh but she was compassionate too and I doubt whether she repeated the practical joke at Reigate Priory!

The evidence of the Account Book

These selected items from the Account Book reveal that the Third Earl sometimes let the Priory, usually for the autumn months.

Expenditure

Oct 7th 1856	Paid Matilda Eade and S Tortoiseshell their board and standing wages and house payments Oct 1st - 6th . . .£17 3s. 7d.
Sept 21st 1857	To Jas Fisher Plumbing, Glazing, Gilding Bookcases, Cleaning and colouring Store-room and Bedroom ceilings, Cleaning and repainting the Iron Gates at both lodges. . . . .£29 5s. 0d.

Income

1854 Dec 2nd	George Wythes - outgoing tenant.
1856 Sept 8th	Lord Vane, recd of him for 4 weeks occupation of the Priory . . . .£100. 0s. 0d. For two tons of coals taken by Lord Vane on entering . . . .£2 18s. 0d.

On July 10th 1857 the Priory was advertised for letting.

Aug 7th	Priory House, recd of Mrs Bethell for 2 months rent . . . .£100 0s. 0d.
Dec 9th	Recd of Mrs Bethell, the third instalment of £300 to 4 Dec '57 . . . .£100 0s. 0d.

1858 Aug 10th Mrs Bethell 2 months
              rent . . . .£100 0s. 0d.
Nov 1st   Mrs Bethell recd of the
              expense of filling the
              ice-house £3 12s. 4d

Mark Dean, a leading 19th century local personality, remembered that George Wythes had both High Trees Farm and Priory Farm, but we have yet to learn more about Lord Vane and Mrs Bethell.

The Jaffray tenancy

Another puzzle was set for us by an American lady from Virginia who visited the Museum in 1979. She assured us that at one time the Priory had belonged to one of her ancestors, John Richmond Jaffray, who died in 1870. As gently as we could, we assured her that the Priory had belonged to the Somers family throughout the 19th century.

On her return home, she posted to us copies of their treasured family pictures. There were portraits of John and Caroline and their son, even a picture of the china they used. Best of all was a group photograph showing the servants all sitting posed in the Priory courtyard - the duplicate of a picture we already had. But written round the edge of the Jaffray copy were the names and positions of the servants - Plummer the old nurse, Hawkins the seamstress, Kate the nursery maid, Morrison the gardener, Scott the coachman and so on. Oliver the butler and the Housekeeper take precedence in the centre as senior servants.

The costumes suggest the 1860s - unfortunately this Account Book finished in 1859 and did not mention the name of Jaffray!

George Nathaniel, Marquess Curzon of Kedleston, Viceroy of India 1899 to 1905, and his first wife, Mary Leiter.

George Nathaniel Curzon

In later years some of the Priory tenants were very well known. George Nathaniel Curzon of Kedleston with his haughty manner and ramrod posture must have made the servants quake in their shoes. He had to wear a corset of leather and steel after suffering from curvature of the spine as a child. When he was at Oxford his undergraduate friends teased him with the lines:-

> 'My name is George Nathaniel Curzon.
> I am a most superior person.
> My cheek is pink, my hair is sleek,
> I dine at Blenheim twice a week.'

He and his charming American wife, Mary Leiter, often rented the Priory from 1896 over about three years. Their second daughter Cynthia, afterwards the wife of Sir Oswald Mosley, was born here only three days after Curzon received the news of his appointment as Viceroy and Governor-General of India. In 1906 Curzon rented the Priory again and entertained here on a lavish scale.

There were other important and

The Priory servants photographed in the courtyard c. 1860.

influential tenants such as Princess Wiasmesky with her two sons in 1901, the Grand Duke Michael of Russia, and General Sir Ian Hamilton.

The Hon. Mrs Ronnie Greville entertains King Edward VII

Perhaps the most flamboyant tenant was the Hon. Mrs Ronnie Greville. Born Margaret Helen, she was the only daughter of the Rt Hon. William McEwan, the Scottish whisky millionaire. In 1891 she married the Hon. Ronald Greville, a captain in the Life Guards, who was a great friend of George Keppel.

Now that she had a place in society, in the Marlborough House circle of King Edward VII, she put all her wits into becoming a great society hostess. The search began for a suitable country house to purchase for their home and as an impressive background for her glittering social gatherings. Meanwhile each year from 1902 to 1906, usually in May, she rented the Priory and entertained leading politicians, writers, artists and even royalty.

Hanging just inside the Priory entrance is a huge photograph taken by a young local photographer, Rowland Sammes. In the visitors' book, on the page dated May 20th 1905, the day of the group photograph, there are the signatures of Edward R. (Edward VII), the Duke and Duchess of Devonshire (the Duchess was known as 'the Old Trout'), Maud Warrender, Arthur Balfour, the Cadogans, Ernest Cassel - the grandfather of Lady Mountbatten, Violet Savile and her husband, Muriel Wilson, William McEwan (Mrs Greville's father) and Alice Keppel, the King's special friend.

Margaret Greville's photographs, pasted into the visitors' book, show the King and his party alighting from their motor car - with hard tyres and open top - at the new main entrance in the courtyard, with the Priory walls covered with ivy. Another shows Margaret Greville's little dog, Tee-to-tum, in front of one of the Priory glass-houses.

In 1906 Mrs Greville found Polesden Lacey, near Dorking, only eight or nine miles from Reigate Priory. She enlarged and furnished the beautiful house to create a perfect background for her

Edward VII at Reigate Priory in 1905. In the back row, the Prime Minister Arthur Balfour, tall and hatless, stands to the King's right. Mr McEwan with the remarkable white beard is in the centre. Mrs Keppel is seated, second from the right of the picture and both Margaret and Ronnie Greville hold their pet dogs.

sumptuous house-parties. Her photographs and visitors' books, many of them relating to the Priory, are now on permanent display in the billiard room there. When Margaret Greville died in 1942 she bequeathed Polesden Lacey, with a suitable endowment, to the National Trust in memory of her father. The Trust have kindly provided us with copies of all their material relating to Reigate Priory.

Visitors to the Somersets

On some of the other pages of the Priory visitors' book are scores of signatures of other well-known personalities, people who came at other times as guests of the Somersets - Winston and Clementine Churchill, John Churchill (Winston's brother), Consuelo Duchess of Marlborough, Alice St Albans (Kitty's mother), Adeline Bedford (Lady Henry Somerset's sister), the Duke and Duchess of Beaufort (Lady Henry's 'in-laws'), Isabel Somerset (Lady Henry herself), Anastasia, Charles and Cicely Bentinck, Lloyd George, Nelly Melba and, again and again, Hilaire Belloc, often with a little drawing or remark, such as 'ex M.P.' in 1911. W B Yeats, Cynthia and Herbert Asquith, Virginia Somers, Austen Chamberlain. The name W Lambton appears frequently too. This was Major-General the Hon. William Lambton, who became Lady Kitty Somerset's second husband in 1921.

Alongside the entry for Aug 27th 1911 Winston wrote the word 'Attaque'. Could this mean that the party enjoyed playing the game of that name, based on military tactics or was there some more subtle significance?

Biographies and diaries are peep-holes into Priory history too. Only two months later Winston was here again - on business. In his book *The World Crisis 1911 - 1918* Churchill described how, in early October 1911, the Prime Minister, Mr Asquith, invited him to become First Sea Lord. Sir John Fisher had retired from the Admiralty following various accusations and criticisms, and Clementine Churchill feared that her husband would find the embittered old man 'a thorn in the flesh'. So she suggested that Winston should tactfully invite Fisher to advise him. They met in the drawing room and Churchill wrote in his diary 'We passed three days together in the comfort of Reigate Priory.'

An interesting snippet comes from the diary of Cynthia Asquith: 'Friday, April 16th 1915 - I caught the four something train from Charing Cross to Reigate and met Evan. He dug me out of my third class and we got into an extraordinary carriage with only one seat in it. We arrived at Reigate Priory soon after five and had tea with Lady Essex, Kitty Somerset and Ava Astor. Conversation mainly was gossip. Ava exquisitely dressed and looking very "larmoyante". She is very beautiful in a decorative Sèvres china way.

'Beb (her husband) arrived and **told** me they really think they are going to the front on Thursday. It is very difficult to believe that history will interfere in one's private life. But going to the front seems too melodramatic to be true.'

Then - two days later - 'Sunday 18th April - When I got out of bed I found my neck and chest were covered with a rash. A little man exactly like Dr Dose in "Happy Families" came to see me, and to my horror and amusement, said he thought it must be **German** Measles. I gnashed my teeth with rage.'

It is clear that Henry Somers Somerset let the Priory frequently and for long periods. During World War I he held responsible Staff positions and served with distinction. By now, Lady Kitty was living separately in London.

Even as this book is being written, and perhaps because of it, reports are emerging which reveal the Priory's rôle at that time. While scouring newspapers for his own research into the history of nearby Redhill, Alan Moore discovered a letter to *The Times* from an American named Irwin Laughlin, dated 2nd December 1933, which gives us a clue:

'I lived at Reigate Priory from 1917 through 1919, during a perilous time when, as Counsellor of the American Embassy, I was struggling against the common enemy and heard from the gardens of the Priory the sound of the guns in Flanders during the attack of March, 1918. A son was born to me there. The beauty and peacefulness of those surroundings helped me immeasurably to carry on through all the accumulated troubles of the last effort of the allies.'

Then we found in a book of memories compiled recently by Women's Institute members, that there was an occasion when the Priory was used as a secret and secure refuge for two future kings, Edward VIII and George VI. The writer's father was a policeman in Reigate.

'Just before I was born there was a big scare about a Sinn Fein plot to murder some members of the Royal Family and the government. The Prince

Bell Street looking southwards to the trees screening the Priory grounds. The little pre-1914 tourer passing the White Hart Hotel has a Leeds registration plate

of Wales, his brother and some of the government ministers were sent down to Reigate Priory in secret and were guarded by the local police. My father was one of these as he had been in the army and could use a gun. He was gone for some time until the scare was over. Afterwards he told my mother he had been guarding the back gate into Bell Street and was most impressed by Churchill, who left by the back gate instead of going back to London with the rest of the party through the main gate.'

The world was now a different place. The era of the great Edwardian house party weekends was over, the 1914-18 war had proved to be truly earth-shattering. But that war had produced another great Admiral, who leads us into the next chapter of Priory history.

SURREY

WITHIN HALF-A-MILE OF REIGATE STATION, TWO MILES FROM REDHILL, 31 MILES FROM BRIGHTON AND 21 MILES BY ROAD FROM LONDON. 15 MINUTES BY CAR FROM WALTON HEATH.

Illustrated Particulars, Plan and Conditions of Sale

of the

Interesting Historical Property

known as

REIGATE PRIORY

dating from the XIIIth Century, and containing the Holbein Hall, a Suite of seven Reception Rooms, 23 Bedrooms; Nurseries, five Bath Rooms and ground floor Offices,

Modern Garage and Stabling, Beautiful Old Gardens and Park Commanding Magnificent Views.

The whole extending to

about **159** Acres

and including a 9-hole Private Golf Course

To be offered in ONE Lot with the

Antique Furniture and Complete Equipment of the House and Gardens

For Sale by Auction by

Messrs. KNIGHT, FRANK & RUTLEY

(Sir Howard G. Frank, K.C.B., John Frederick Knight, Alfred J. Burrows, Arthur Horace Knight)

at the ESTATE ROOM, 20, HANOVER SQUARE, LONDON, W.1, on TUESDAY, 9th SEPTEMBER, 1919, at 2.30 o'clock precisely (unless previously sold).

Land Agent :	*Solicitors :*	*Auctioneers' Offices :*
Major A. Roger Rowden, Old Town Hall, Reigate.	Messrs. Trower, Still, Parkin & Keeling, 5, New Square, Lincoln's-Inn-Fields, W.C.2.	20, Hanover Square, W.1 ; 41, Bank Street, Ashford, Kent'; 100, Princes Street, Edinburgh ; and 78, St. Vincent Street, Glasgow.

Reigate Priory had been on the market for two years when Admiral and Countess Beatty bought the house and gardens in August 1921. They were attracted by the stabling, the grazing land and by the historic connection with Charles Howard, the great Lord High Admiral of Armada fame. The wooded ridge, known as Reigate Park, had been bought by Randal Vogan for presentation to the people of Reigate.

THE BEATTYS
- THE ADMIRAL, THE MILLIONAIRESS AND THE DERBY WINNER

T he Beattys have a unique rôle in our story, for though they made few changes to the building and took only a small part in Reigate affairs, they were - as far as we know - to be the last private owners of Reigate Priory.

From our invaluable Priory visitors' book we discover that David and Ethel Beatty were guests here in November 1912, when they came to join a small weekend house party given by Henry and Kitty Somerset.

Even at that time David Beatty had already made his mark, for at 41 he had risen to be the youngest Flag Officer in the Royal Navy since the time of Nelson. Winston Churchill as First Lord of the Admiralty was impressed by Beatty's outstanding brilliance and selected him to be his Naval Secretary.

Like the great Lord High Admiral Charles Howard of Effingham, owner of Reigate Priory three centuries earlier, Beatty had saved his country from invasion and from defeat at sea. He was a national hero and a legend in his own time.

Admiral Beatty's life is comprehensively documented in at least three excellent biographies. His letters and diaries have been published and there are collections of contemporary newspapers, both national and local, which describe his career.

Another archive of photographs and artefacts is held by the Imperial War Museum. It was there we made an amusing discovery - Joey, the Admiral's bulldog, survives to this day (stuffed) in their reserve collection at Duxford.

David and Ethel Beatty

David Beatty was born in 1871, into an old Irish family which had settled in England and was very well known in hunting and racing circles. Throughout his life he took a great interest in training and breeding good horses - riding was always his chief recreation.

When he was only twelve years old he entered the Naval Academy at Gosport, then proceeded to pass every examination with distinction. His progress was meteoric.

But in 1901, when he had reached the rank of Captain, Beatty risked his whole naval career by

David Beatty – from a crayon portrait by John Sargent R.A. in 1919.

Ethel Beatty – from a portrait by Philip de Laszlo in 1911.

marrying an elegant and wealthy divorcee, whom he had met on the hunting field. Mrs Ethel Tree, one of the wealthiest women in England, was the only daughter of the multi-millionaire Marshall Field, the American chain-store pioneer. She had obtained a divorce from her first husband, who was living in America with their one little son.

Royal etiquette at that time would not allow any divorced person to be presented at Court and no divorced woman would be received in society. Most naval officers in this situation found themselves forced to resign. But when Queen Victoria died and Edward VII came to the throne there was a loosening of many conventions and, after all, Ethel Tree's divorce was only for desertion. So over a few years, the scandal died quietly away. The Beattys had many good friends, they themselves entertained lavishly and soon, in turn, the Beattys found themselves fully accepted everywhere.

There is the story that, soon after the Beattys were married and were in quarters in Malta, he damaged his ship's engines in his haste to get back to harbour from sea. When, as a result, he was threatened with court martial, Ethel declared 'What! Court martial my David? I'll buy them a new ship!'

By 1913 he was in command of the Battle Cruiser

Squadron and during the 1914-18 war, as Vice-Admiral Sir David Beatty, from the deck of his famous flagship HMS *Lion,* he led his battle cruisers to victory on many occasions and sank a large number of German ships.

The climax came in May 1916, when he forced the German High Seas Fleet into the jaws of Admiral Jellicoe's British Grand Fleet. The German fleet suffered badly in the famous Battle of Jutland which followed, though the British fleet came off badly too, for many of the ships exploded. This was the occasion of Beatty's famous understatement - 'There seems to be something wrong with our ships today!'. He was right, the armour of the British ships was not strong enough to protect their magazines.

The battle of Jutland was indecisive, but the German fleet lost heart and limped home and never engaged in force again. In 1918 it was Beatty who accepted their surrender on the deck of his new flagship, HMS *Queen Elizabeth.* The German ships were escorted to Scapa Flow and scuttled by their own crews. In 1919 the British Government rewarded Beatty with £100,000, he was created an Earl and he was made Admiral of the Fleet and First Sea Lord. His fighting days at sea were over, but from that time David Beatty worked mainly at the Admiralty in London, with the massive responsibility of administering and re-organising the British fleet. He was provided with an official Admiralty residence, the Mall House in Admiralty Arch.

Admiral of the Fleet Sir David Beatty on the quarter deck of H.M.S. Queen Elizabeth.

The Beattys owned a number of properties. After renting Brooksby Hall in Leicestershire for some years as a hunting lodge, they purchased the property in 1911, and Ethel Beatty established an excellent stable there. When David Beatty was created Earl he also became Viscount Borodale of Wexford and Baron Beatty of the North Sea and of Brooksby. The Hall is now a College for Further Education and the stables have been developed for use as an Equestrian Centre. Grantully Castle, near Aberfeldy in Scotland, was rented each year for the shooting season.

In wartime, while the Fleet was based on the Firth of Forth, the Beattys rented Aberdour House near Rosyth, where they could provide some social life for officers and snatch a little time together. Ethel Beatty also owned a large sea-going yacht named *Sheelah*, which during the war she had fitted out, no expense spared, as a hospital. She engaged leading surgeons and well qualified nurses and worked devotedly herself caring for injured sailors and organising great fund-raising efforts to support their families.

In London, as a base for formal entertaining and visiting the theatre, the Beattys owned first Hanover Lodge near Regent's Park, and later 17 Grosvenor Square.

But life in London, then as now, was very noisy and stressful. Ethel Beatty had everything that money could buy, and a husband who loved her deeply, but she resented his long absences and suffered increasingly from depression.

The Countess longed for the peace of the country - so now that her husband would be working mainly in London, they looked for a retreat within easy reach of the Admiralty, but where they could relax informally and enjoy a settled family life with their two boys, David born in 1905 and Peter in 1910. They could keep a few horses, they could ride - and perhaps Ethel Beatty's health would improve.

Reigate Priory was just what was needed, only 21 miles from London, in a pleasant old town set in beautiful countryside.

In 1921, nine years after their first visit, the Beattys drove again down Park Lane, past the Priory's north lodge, through the handsome wrought iron gateway, down the tree-lined drive, between the eagles perched on their pillars and round to the courtyard door. This time David came not only as a full-blown Admiral but with the dignity of an Earl.

Now Beatty and his Countess were coming to take up possession as the new owners of Reigate Priory.

The Beattys come to the Priory

Many reports say that it was the Countess who bought Reigate Priory - but in *The Times* on 7th May 1921, under the headline 'Lord Beatty's New Home' came the news 'Reigate Priory has been sold by Mr Somers Somerset to Lord and Lady Beatty, who will take up their residence there at an early date'. The conveyance document is dated later, on 23rd August 1921, and says that Reigate Priory, the mansion with 68½ acres of land, was sold by Henry Somers Somerset to the Rt. Hon. David Earl Beatty GCB, OM, GCVO, DSO for £35,000. Officially, therefore, the purchaser was Earl Beatty, but it is more than likely that it was his wife Ethel who made the money available.

In 1922, only a few months later, the Admiral wrecked his car in Park Lane not far from the Priory when he swerved to avoid a cyclist. His breast bone was broken, leading to recurring chest trouble.

The people of Reigate were pleased and proud to welcome these famous and wealthy new owners, but the relationship between town and Priory had now undergone a subtle change. Following the Great Sale of Reigate, the owner of the Priory was no longer the Lord of the Manor, nor the landlord of much of the town. It was most fortunate that the Priory and its estate were to be purchased as one unit, in the care of a family which would maintain it with distinction.

The gardens were now well designed and established, with facilities for golf, tennis and croquet. Though the wooded greensand ridge was now open to the public and fenced off from the Priory grounds, the band of forest trees made a beautiful backdrop to the view southwards from the Priory's main windows.

The house had been refurbished and extended fairly recently and no structural improvements were needed, but the big room between the two courtyards was converted into a billiard room, with one part fitted up as a workshop - for the Admiral liked to do a little carpentry sometimes. More bathrooms, lavatories, telephones and lifts were installed. It was at this time that Lady Henry Somerset's heraldic stained glass was removed from the windows over the grand staircase. How we wish we knew where it went!

The Priory house was, however, quite empty. The Somers and Somerset family treasures, portraits of the ancestors and the heirlooms had been taken to Eastnor Castle and Badminton House. Everything else, from the exquisite Louis Seize commode of Kingwood in the Drawing Room to the last hip bath from the bothy, had been sold in the five sale days held the previous June. So Countess Beatty spent lavishly on the complete refurnishing and restocking of the mansion.

Staff were needed too, at least 20 to run the house. Excellent staff accommodation was available in the new east wing built by Lady Henry Somerset. Seven or eight gardeners were needed to maintain the grounds. There were the grooms, the stable-boys and the chauffeurs, who lived over the stables and garages in the outer courtyard. The Priory laundry in Park Lane required its own staff of five or six for it was a self-contained unit which dealt not only with the laundry from the Priory, but coped with the laundry which came by train, in great wicker hampers, from all the other Beatty properties. There were cottages around the estate, where the dairyman, the park keeper or the lodge keeper lived. The Priory formed a little world of its own.

Living Memory

But to give us the atmosphere and the little details of everyday life, there are, in Reigate and scattered around the world, people who still have vivid memories of the days when they worked for the Beattys. Over the years, many of them have come back to see the Priory and we have taken every opportunity to record their memories.

Then in 1995 Carolyn Burnley produced her excellent videotape *Reigate Priory 1921-48*, which captures not only memories but personalities.

Dorothy Alltimes was second housemaid from 1922 to 1925 and remembered the Admiral's cherished mementoes, two ship's lanterns in the Grand Dining Room, the name-plate of HMS *Lion* let into the hearth of one of the fireplaces, and Nelson's famous message 'England expects …' framed in flags and hanging on the upstairs landing. She remembers too the gardener's cottage on the estate which was used at times by an antiques dealer, employed by the Countess to go all over the country to buy antiques for furnishing her various properties.

Josephine Fueggle now lives near her daughter in Ontario, but came back to the Priory a few years ago while visiting relations in Reigate. As we showed her around the Priory as it is today the memories came flooding back - especially the night she sat on the backstairs because the newly installed central heating pipes made her little room as hot as an oven. She recognised the wallpaper in one of the attic rooms, still in place.

Josephine's maiden name was Aherne and she worked as a 'travelling housemaid' for the Beattys from 1927 to 1931. She spent at least six weeks of each year at the Priory during Ascot and told us that working for the Beattys was the most memorable time of her life, for they treated their staff extremely well. She remembered the little cottage on the Priory estate where a Mr and Mrs Revel lived. 'They made the cream, butter and cheese for the Priory household. As a little boy, Peter Beatty often stayed at the cottage with the Revels and thought the world of them, so much so that later, when he bought Mereworth Castle, he gave them the south wing to live in when they retired.'

Alice Walter was a third housemaid at the Priory, but she had to go occasionally to other Beatty houses. Alice was a Welsh girl who came to Reigate at the age of 17. She saw an advert for a housemaid in the window of La Trobes' shop in the Market Place, went to the Priory for an interview and was taken on. 'We earned about £100 a year', she said. 'We had to provide our own uniforms, checked dress plus cap and apron for the morning, and navy blue for the afternoon. The food was lovely and we were never short of anything. Housemaids were waited on too and didn't even have to wash up.'

When the Beattys were in residence she had to get up at 6.30. The servants were not allowed to be seen downstairs, so all the cleaning of grates, dusting and polishing had to be done before the family came down for breakfast.

While working at the Priory, Alice met her future husband, a mechanic at the garage just round the corner in Bell Street. This was the garage which supplied and serviced the Beatty cars - the Admiral's Daimler, the Countess' Rolls-Royce and, later on, the sports cars for their sons - David, Lord Borodale and the Hon. Peter Beatty.

Alice left the Priory to work in Yorkshire for a few years, but she missed Frank, so returned to take a housemaid's place at Gatton Hall. Frank and Alice married in 1939, and in the 1980s, to Alice's delight, her grandsons Steve and Lee came to Reigate Priory as pupils at the Priory Middle School.

Different memories are recalled by **Mr Sherry Legg** who comes from a family which has been in Reigate since 1725 and has helped to maintain the house and estate for five generations.

When they worked at the Priory in the 1920s, one of their responsibilities was to maintain the boundary fencing around the estate, starting from the end of the old wall in Bell Street, up the hill, along the edge of the woods, to divide Reigate Park from the Priory grounds, then up Park Lane back to the woodyard near the north gateway.

There was a fascinating mystique about life behind the Priory's six foot high, close-boarded fence and many local people confess to peeping through the knot holes and cracks, but there were odd occasions - in wintry weather - when the 'swarf' was swept from the ice on the lake, braziers were set up on the bank and lights were hung from the trees. Then, when the ice had been tested by driving a farm cart from one bank to the other, some local people were invited to come in and enjoy the skating.

It was Sherry Legg's grandfather who constructed the circular pool in the sunk garden and made the trammel to shape the plaster surround. The pool is now planted out as a flower bed and the trammel survived until fairly recently.

Mr Legg remembers the 'ha-ha', the deep ditch which was lined on the north side with a brick wall, to prevent grazing animals from damaging the gardens. The line of the ha-ha is now followed by the main east to west path from the children's play park to the lake. In earlier days there would have been deer, then sheep and cattle on the open grassland, but with the coming of the Beattys, horses took precedence, so an extra fence was erected above the wall of the ha-ha, to provide the additional height which would keep them out.

The Leggs did inside work too. The small dining room which had been painted pale blue and had a simple classical style during the Somers era, was now to be transformed by marbling. The floor of thick old boards was painstakingly worked on by Mr Legg until every knot and nail was treated and it was as smooth as glass. Next it was divided into 2' squares, and painted by skilled Italian workmen until it looked exactly like thick tiles of marble. Sherry and his father maintained this floor through the Beatty years, restoring it with heavy floor varnish when necessary.

In the middle of this room stood a marble dining table, with a beautiful crystal chandelier hanging

A picture postcard sent to a friend by one of the domestic staff. We can just see the brick ha-ha, built to protect the gardens from the animals in the park, without destroying the view.

above. Alice Walter clearly remembers one day when she was cleaning window-sills and the head housemaid was washing the crystals. Suddenly there was a loud crash - the chandelier collapsed onto the marble table. Fortunately the damage to the table was repaired successfully by Marriages, the hardware and ironmongery firm in Bell Street.

Many years ago, **Ellen Selsby**, a local policeman's widow who had been one of Lady Beatty's housemaids in 1922, found the pencilled list she had made of Priory guests at that time - Lord Birkenhead who had been Lord Chancellor and was to become Secretary of State for India, Lord Winterton who became Father of the House of Commons, the Churchills, Mr and Mrs Marshall Field, the Duke of York who became King George VI and his brother Prince George, the Duke of Kent who was killed in World War II. Josephine Fueggle remembers Sir Algernon Blackwood, Diana Fellowes, Jessie Matthews the film star and King Alfonso of Spain. All these people obviously counted the Beattys as their friends and enjoyed their hospitality at the Priory.

News reports show the level of their social life in London - 'The King and Queen honoured Admiral of the Fleet Earl Beatty and Countess Beatty with their Company at dinner last night at Grosvenor Square...'. 'The Queen wore a gown of white and silver at Countess Beatty's dinner party on Thursday. The King took his hostess in to dinner...'

Another report is a little surprising - 'The new ice rink is becoming decidedly fashionable. On looking in there recently I saw Lady Beatty, Mrs Alan Adare and the beautiful Lady Brecknock, who have temporarily deserted the hunting field.'

Another glimpse of the Beattys comes, not from a newspaper this time, but in the minutes of a local club for May 9th, 1927. 'New members elected to Reigate Heath Golf Club, Earl Beatty, Countess Beatty, Lord Borodale and Hon. Peter Beatty'. There is a little revelation about Admiral Beatty's golf in Lord Chatfield's autobiography *The Navy and Defence*. 'Beatty liked golf and took many opportunities of playing, but he played only moderately. A wound sustained in China affected his left hand and his grip of the club, but he played down to 10 handicap. Clenching his teeth he would smite the ball furiously, not always down the fairway.'

Lord Chatfield, as Beatty's flag captain on the *Lion,* grew to know the Admiral and his wife very well. He wrote 'I got many insights into Beatty's personality - its strength, its audacity, the impossibility of throwing him off his balance, his power of extricating himself from difficult positions'.

There is a collection of letters edited by W S Chalmers, many of them from David Beatty to his wife, and from them we make an interesting discovery. Ethel Beatty's nature was, we know, very restless. They had been at Reigate Priory only about 18 months when, on 4th March 1923, David Beatty wrote 'As regards the Priory, I quite understand you don't like it and are anxious to get rid of it. But you cannot get rid of it in a hurry unless you are prepared to lose a very large sum of money. Your fault is that you always want to do things in a hurry.'

But she did sell Hanover Lodge - then the Countess changed her mind. In February 1925 Beatty wrote to her 'It was done at your express wish, and what is done can't be undone... We can manage quite well in the Mall House and at the Priory once the weather improves.'

The following year, on December 5th 1926, while the family and a large house party were at dinner, a fire broke out in the Priory roof, fortunately not in the historic part of the house, but above the workshop. The men of the party stripped off their jackets and manned the fire hoses, so there was no serious damage - only singeing of the roof timbers and saturated furniture and carpets.

A later book, *Our Admiral*..., written by a nephew, Charles Beatty, gives us more cheerful and colourful impressions of life at the Priory. He describes the Grand Dining Room with its gold leaf ceiling. 'The effect was fantastic, since every article on the table, candlesticks, spoons and forks seemed to be solid gold.' We suspect that this wonderful ceiling, created for Lady Henry Somerset with her initials moulded in plaster, was extravagantly transformed to Countess Beatty's taste, with the application of gold leaf. Pictures in the 1921 Sale Book, and earlier pictures, show the ceiling without gilding.

He describes too how Ethel Beatty acquired one of the first electric gramophones, called a Panotrope. 'Disguised as a piece of antique furniture, it stood by the newel post at the bottom of the grand staircase in the Priory's biggest room. The machine had a huge output and frequently rocked the dignified shades with "jazz".'

Admiral Beatty had his own frivolities too. On one occasion, when his wife was away, he invited the whole Gaiety Chorus to a party at the Priory. Collected reminiscences give us the impression that Admiral Beatty certainly had 'an eye for the ladies'.

Ethel Beatty made a great effort to conquer her depression and took great pains with her appearance. She showed Charles Beatty how she set about acquiring the latest fashions - 'Before each season came round, the grand couturier, Worth, designed for her whatever garment she specified for morning, noon or night. Transferring his ideas to fabric, pinned on a mannequin of her build and colouring, they were then sketched, hand coloured and bound in an elegant folder. The one she showed me at Reigate contained perhaps twenty plates in water-colours. Having brooded on the plates, all she had to do was to note the "number" she approved, along with any changes which took her fancy, and perhaps this was the origin of the enduring habit of referring to Paris originals as "numbers" - such as "the little black number".'

Charles Beatty describes too how Ethel Beatty arranged for a Scottish piper to parade the full length of the Priory's south front, playing at full blast at eight o'clock each morning!

Reigate people saw little of the Beattys. The Earl's most memorable public appearances were on Sunday, August 5th 1923 when he unveiled the Borough's war memorial at Shaw's Corner, and later, on the same afternoon, marched at the head of the British Legion to the Memorial Sports Ground in Redhill, then declared it open and made a rousing speech.

In the photographs taken on these occasions the Admiral is unmistakeable, with his cap still at a jaunty angle and his bulldog jaw firm and determined.

He served as First Sea Lord until 1927 and on August 1st he wrote to a friend, from Reigate Priory 'It is all over, I've left my office... it is very peaceful here'.

From this time they spent longer periods each year at the Priory, but they bought yet another country house. Not far from Brooksby Hall in Leicestershire's hunting country they found Dingley Hall, an interesting and attractive mansion set in extensive grounds. Like Reigate Priory it had been founded in the thirteenth century as a religious house.

Unfortunately, Countess Beatty's health continued to deteriorate and no treatment could be found to save her. She died, as a result of a cerebral thrombosis, at Dingley Hall in the spring of 1932. The Admiral died only four years later in March 1936.

Though suffering from a chest infection himself, he had recently attended the funerals of two of his closest friends, Admiral Jellicoe and King George V. He had wished to be buried beside his wife at Dingley, but the country insisted on a state funeral; his coffin was laid close to that of Lord Nelson, in the crypt of St Paul's Cathedral.

Twelve years later, in 1948 - the long delay was caused by World War II - an impressive ceremony was held in Trafalgar Square on Trafalgar Day, 21st October. Two splendid busts were unveiled to commemorate these two great World War I Admirals, Jellicoe and Beatty. Six cadets and one officer were invited to represent the Reigate Sea Cadet Unit at this ceremony, for Earl Beatty had for a time been their President.

The Hon. Peter Beatty

Naturally, when Admiral Earl Beatty died, it was his elder son David, Lord Borodale, who inherited the earldom, along with Brooksby Hall. Reigate Priory came to his younger son Peter, together with a considerable fortune.

Peter Beatty's great talent was in breeding and training horses and his racing successes brought him both satisfaction and large winnings. In 1938 he

was the winner of the Derby with his horse Bois Roussel, and in the same year he won the Ascot Gold Vase with Foxglove 2, a horse he had bought from the Aga Khan only 24 hours before the race.

Unfortunately Peter Beatty was born with sight in only one eye and the sight in the other deteriorated until he was ultimately blind. Races had to be described to him by friends. He relied a lot on his German Shepherd dog Binnie, who was trained as a guard dog and probably acted as a guide dog too.

Though Peter Beatty owned stables and a house at Newmarket, his first priority on becoming owner of Reigate Priory was to build the new range of stabling near the Park Lane entrance. Over the years, many successful horses have been housed here. Most recently the stables were run by Jack Donaghue who trained many horses owned by Queen Elizabeth, the Queen Mother. In 1997 the buildings were sold for conversion into desirable homes.

It was Peter Beatty who had the open air swimming pool built. It was designed by Vincent Hooper, lined with blue tiles, equipped with a pump and filter room. This pool has now been made shallower, and is used in the summertime as a children's paddling pool.

Peter Beatty had granted the tenancy of the Priory to Joseph Rank Ltd until six months after the end of the war, then in 1942 he decided to sell it. He retained the Priory Stable, the grounds and a suite of rooms for his own use.

In 1944 he bought Mereworth Castle near Maidstone - a splendid home - which he could not fully enjoy due to his loss of sight. On October 27th 1949 the *Daily Telegraph* reported:

'The Hon. Peter Beatty, son of the late Admiral of the Fleet, Earl Beatty, who inherited two fortunes and was a successful racehorse owner, had one shadow over his life - the threat of total blindness.

'Mr Beatty, who was 39, had consulted many specialists. Yesterday he left his first floor suite at the Ritz Hotel Piccadilly W1, saying he was going to see a friend on the sixth floor. A few minutes later he fell to his death in the courtyard.'

When Peter Beatty sold the estate to the Insurance Company in 1942, he leased the area enclosed by the dark dotted line on this map. Though now he lived mainly in London or at Mereworth Castle near Maidstone, Reigate was a convenient location for his horses, with easy access for racing at Epsom and Ascot

THE PRIORY IN WARTIME

O n 27th October 1939, a few weeks after the outbreak of World War II, this short notice appeared in the *Surrey Mirror*:-

'On behalf of the Hon. Peter Beatty, the Reigate Priory has been let for the duration of the war to Joseph Rank Ltd. The mansion is to be used as emergency offices in connection with the control of wheat.'

Though Joseph Rank did not own Reigate Priory, he was a man who should be remembered. From his humble origins in Hull, as the son of a miller who owned one small windmill, he went on to modernise the whole of the country's flour milling industry.

Joseph Rank always lived modestly and regarded his wealth as a trust. He was a deeply religious man who supported Methodism both nationally and locally, giving generously wherever he saw a need. In 1931 he came to live at Colley Corner, Reigate Heath, less than a mile from Reigate Priory.

His second son, J Arthur Rank, settled at Reigate Heath too, at the large house named Heathfield. He was a pillar of the Reigate Methodist Church, and the splendid magic lantern which he used to illustrate his Sunday school lessons is now in the care of our Priory Museum.

The Control of Wheat in wartime

Reigate Priory offered all that Joseph Rank Ltd needed - rooms of different sizes for offices, facilities for catering and recreation, and sleeping accommodation for some of the employees whose homes were in London. A small staff remained at Rank's head office in Leadenhall Street in Central London, but about 160 came to work at the Priory.

Peter Beatty retained a few rooms in the Priory for his own use and continued to use the stables and much of the park for grazing his horses.

Most of the cellar area beneath the Priory's Holbein Hall was strengthened by filling it with concrete, though one section (still accessible and now used for storing cleaning materials) was adapted for use as an air-raid shelter, complete with lavatories. Many of Peter Beatty's pictures, quantities of plate and other valuables were stored in the cellar reached from the trapdoor which is still under the main staircase.

I wonder, could it have been at this time that Sir John Parsons' splendid brass chandelier was lifted from its hook above the staircase and stored for safety? Earlier pictures show it in place, but where it is now we have no idea. It may be inscribed like its twin which still hangs in the Parish Church, so, who knows? one day it might be found, identified and perhaps returned.

Some of the people who came with Rank to work here in Reigate come to visit our Museum, and some are featured in Carolyn Burnley's excellent video-tape. Their reminiscences give us a comprehensive insight into life at the Priory in wartime.

Four air-raid shelters were built in the grounds and the swimming pool was kept filled for use as a static water tank. The Ministry of Defence used the areas under the trees for parking armoured vehicles and storing fuel. Some people remember a barrage balloon floating above the area and on one occasion a Canadian unit camped beside the lake - but only for 48 hours.

Now follows a tale of an exciting recent discovery. While clearing the tangle of sheds and buildings for the supermarket development early in the 1990s, a rusty wrought iron gateway came to light. Fortunately, a technical book on wrought iron

After 250 years, Sir John Parsons' gateway from Park Lane had to be removed, when a Canadian army vehicle damaged the intricate wrought ironwork. The rusting remains came to light only recently.

work identified it as the gate from the Priory's Park Lane entrance, which had been missing since the time of the war.

We are told that the gates had been damaged by a Canadian armoured car, so they were dismantled, stored for safety and forgotten. Now they are in the Borough's care, awaiting restoration. Then they will be either rehung or displayed somewhere in the Priory building.

Brian Flint, one of our visitors, remembers rows of camouflaged Nissen huts under the trees too. Brian was only 14 when he came to the Priory as a clerk. He remembers that the staircase pillars and the Holbein fireplace were boarded up for protection and he makes two confessions - occasionally he helped himself to peaches from the walled kitchen garden - and once he actually cycled the whole length of the long corridor in the Priory's east wing - from the baize door, past the canteen and kitchens and down to the boot hole.

Sometimes the building was filled with delicious smells of baking bread, coming from the laboratory upstairs - when samples of flour were being tested.

Basil Allison was one of the staff who came with Ranks from London, when he was 17. He stayed with the firm until he retired at 60. He recalls the sleeping arrangements. 70 or 80 people had to live in, so there were seven or eight to a room, fewer for senior staff. The ladies' and gentlemen's quarters were separate - of course - with a 'chastity door' of plywood fitted across a corridor. 'This caused great fun' he said, 'but it was respected'.

On the ground floor the library was the registration room, where all Rank shareholders were registered. The drawing room next to it was the book-keeping department, where the accounts were kept of every transaction involving the purchase of flour. The central Holbein Hall housed the general office, with the post department in the space under the grand staircase.

What is now the narrower part of the main hall was then a separate room. This was the small dining room which housed the insurance and invoicing departments - models of efficiency. In the study opposite were the Secretary (for some time Miss Troughton, who still lives in Reigate), and her staff. Joseph Rank's office was the old boudoir - now the school office.

The grand dining room with the gold ceiling was still used for meals, but the tapestry-covered walls were protected by heavy gold curtains. Sometimes, in the long dark winter evenings, the furniture was stacked against the walls and dances were held here, with music from an old wind-up gramophone, placed on a collapsible card table in the middle of the room. Echoes of Lady Beatty ten years earlier?

In the rooms leading from the long corridor were more typists, the transport department and the telephonists. The lofty, light and airy kitchen, thoughtfully provided for her servants by Lady Henry Somerset 40 years earlier, was now reigned over by a Mr Wadey and the food he cooked on the massive coal range was good and plentiful, in spite of wartime rationing. Most of the fruit and vegetables came fresh from the Priory gardens, grown by two elderly gardeners, past call-up age. Some of the apples from the Priory orchards were sold to the staff, though there is more than a hint that some were 'scrumped'.

Basil Allison has some more vivid memories of those days:

For weeks there was an abominable smell in the library. Drains were renewed and every possible cause explored, at great expense and with no success; eventually when Mr Allison leaned over a desk illuminated by a desk lamp with a cracked bakelite shade, the smell was so intense that he realised he had found the cause.

He remembers that 'Near the swimming pool there was a revolving summer house, an ideal place for a young man to take a young lady to read a book or admire the scenery or something. It was an

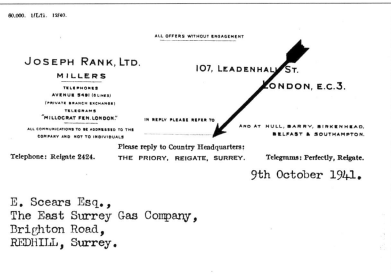

This letter from Ernest Scears' research material reveals his interest in the Priory over many years.

unwritten rule that when they left they would turn the summer house round so that you could see it was empty.'

Mr Allison says he will never forget when a bomb dropped nearby during an air raid. A rather large chap called Ffinch dived under his knee-hole desk and it was extremely difficult to extricate him, like extracting a cork from a bottle.

He remembers fire-watching rotas, four men at a time, based in a bedroom up in the top floor. When the air raid siren went, they patrolled the roof to deal with any incendiary bombs, with buckets of sand, water and stirrup pumps at the ready. They must have done their job well, for there is no record of wartime damage to the building.

To the Ratepayers and Residents of the Borough of Reigate.

A PUBLIC MEETING

will be held in the

Boys' Grammar School Hall,

REIGATE ROAD, REIGATE, on

FRIDAY, NOVEMBER 24th, at 7.30 p.m.

to consider the Public Acquisition of the

REIGATE PRIORY
ESTATE AND HOUSE.

Chairman : Major H. A. HARMAN, D.S.O.,
Chairman of the Executive Committee, Borough Youth Council.

Speakers :

Brig.-General P. MAUD,
Chairman of the Grounds and Layout Committee of the National Playing Fields Association.

Miss AITKEN, M.A.,
Head Mistress, County School for Girls.

Councillor W. J. CLARKE, and a RATEPAYER.

Discussion Invited.

The Priory could provide a Public Branch Library ; a Community Centre ; Playing Fields for the Young People of the Borough and the Elementary School Children.

THE HOLMESDALE PRESS LTD., REDHILL

This meeting was packed to capacity. With only one dissentient those attending voted to support the acquisition of the whole of the Priory estate by the Borough of Reigate.

The Crusader Insurance Company

Another London firm which found war-time office space in Reigate was the Mutual Property Life and General Insurance Company - later to be renamed the Crusader Insurance Company. They were using Woodhatch Lodge, another mansion about half a mile to the south-east of the Priory.

When Peter Beatty decided in 1942 to sell the Priory the Insurance Company were the purchasers. The lease arrangements made by the flour millers, Joseph Rank, Ltd, would continue until six months after the end of the war and Peter Beatty would continue to lease the Priory Stable, the grounds and his suite of rooms.

The Council to the rescue!

Gradually the wider implications of the change from private ownership were creating deep consternation amongst the people of Reigate. In 1943 someone blew the gaff and they learned that a town bypass was being considered, to cut straight across the Priory grounds. There were plans for developing the remaining land as a housing estate and for building shops on the Bell Street frontage. The Priory building might be adapted for use as the Company's head office.

At once, letters of protest were written to the council and to the local and national newspapers, and public meetings were held.

One of these letters came from Mr Ernest Lancashire who was the Secretary of the Workers' Educational Association. He suggested that after the war the Borough should buy the Priory estate, for laying out public pleasure grounds and playing fields especially for young people, and that the building should be used as a Civic Centre, for Adult Education or as a Community Centre.

The insurance company reluctantly agreed they might be willing to sell the estate - but with the exception of the Bell Street frontage, which they wished to retain as a permanent investment.

Many similar letters supported Mr Lancashire's views, though a few people expressed their concern that more housing was urgently needed, and their opposition to a rise in the rates to finance the Priory project. Mrs Lancashire has recently donated to the Priory Museum a most useful addition to our archives, her husband's collection of newspaper cuttings concerning the preservation of the Priory.

Ernest Lancashire, the artist Frank Potter and Stanley Peck formed a powerful little discussion group which met frequently in the sitting room of Mr Peck's home in West Street. With great enthusiasm and determination they missed no opportunity to win support from such well known figures as Chuter Ede, a national figure and one of Surrey's most effective politicians. They enlisted help from local councillors and 'the man in the street', believing, rightly, that community spirit and public co-operation could achieve success. Borough Council meetings were fully attended when the proposals were discussed, and gradually the practicalities for saving the Priory were worked out.

The enthusiasm of this group led a few years later to the formation of the Reigate Society, 'to preserve all natural and architectural beauty within the locality of Reigate'. Its first meeting was held at the Priory on May 23rd 1952 and its first immediate concern at that time was centred on the Priory itself, both for the mansion and for the park.

Already the group's efforts had persuaded the local Council that the Priory must be saved. In 1944 the Greater London Plan designated Reigate Priory as Local Green Belt and in 1946 the Priory Estate was zoned as Public Open Space. When the insurance company appealed the Minister of Town and Country Planning replied 'The Minister is convinced that the Priory Estate, uniquely situated in relation to the town of Reigate and with Park and Mansion designed as and welded through the centuries into a separate entity, merits preservation as a whole, and that it should not be broken up by any building development whatsoever'.

Sixteen acres of the grounds were sold outright to Surrey County Council for playing fields, but they were not to be fenced in and the grounds were to be 'kept in the character of a gentleman's park'. The Priory mansion was to be readily accessible to the people of Reigate, but the arrangements for its purchase proved to be rather complicated.

The days of private ownership were over, and now the whole of the ancient beautiful park was to be open for everyone to enjoy. The building was to play a greater part in the life of local people than ever before.

School dinners in the Holbein Hall in the mid-1970s.
The bronze figure of Margot Fonteyn, by Nathan David, was displayed here for a time.

REIGATE PRIORY BECOMES A SCHOOL

How did Reigate Priory become a school?

The Priory could be used to solve a problem.

The 1944 Education Act had decreed that, after the age of eleven, all children were to enter 'Secondary Schools' and the leaving age was to be raised from 14 to 15 years.

So suitable buildings were needed for the children of the additional year. In Redhill some existing school buildings could be adapted, but none could be found in Reigate. Following the war, money and materials for building were limited, and the need was urgent.

Mr H.E.Collinson, the headmaster of Earlswood School, found a solution. He was aware that Reigate Priory had become an embarrassment to the commercial firm which had been prevented from developing the estate. He knew that the Borough was under strong pressure to acquire the building for community use, but could not afford to buy it.

One wintry day in 1946 Mr Collinson came to see the Priory for himself. The building was empty and derelict. Cisterns in the roof had burst because of the frosts and he had to wade through inches of water on the ground floor.

In spite of these conditions he was convinced that the Priory could happily house a school, and so with the backing of the County Inspector of Schools and the Chief Education Officer, Mr Collinson cautiously presented these ideas to the Borough and the County. Gradually they won support. The Mayor set up a Priory Fund, inviting gifts from the public, Surrey County Council made a sizeable loan, the Ministry of Education agreed to contribute. The buildings became the property of the Borough, but they were to be put in order and maintained by the County, for use as a school.

At first an arrangement was made for the school to use the ground floor rooms for only two years, and the upper floor rooms for ten years. The whole building could be used in the evenings by the Borough.

This unusual arrangement was made to work though it created some knotty problems legally and financially. The school soon needed more space, so after a time a lease was negotiated to last until 1995, with most of the building used by the school in the daytime. Now a new lease lasts until 2120!

Mr F E Claytor, headmaster of the Priory Secondary School, 1948-57.

Reigate Priory County Secondary School

In September 1948 the new school opened with 140 boys and girls aged 13 and 14 - six classes and six teachers. Mr F.E.Claytor was appointed to be the first headmaster, with Miss Brewer as his deputy.

Mr Claytor wrote about those early days in an article for *Priory News*, the excellent school magazine which ran for about 20 years. He remembered helping Mr Higgins, the first caretaker, to sweep out the derelict rooms. 'The Priory was still very much the ghost of an old mansion', he said.

'The old kitchen, to be used as the Art Room, still had the old coal-fired ovens all along one wall and, in the meat store, where the boys' toilets were to be constructed, there were still the butcher's rails and hooks for six carcasses.

'Stalls, tether hooks and feeding racks remained in the stable between the two courtyards. Upstairs, scattered over the building, were various bathrooms, but no hot water. At intervals in the corridors were bell indicators which had long ceased to function, and I have often looked at the discs showing "Her Ladyship's Bathroom" and wondered which bell-push formerly worked it. The rope-hauled lift was still in working order up on

Mr Chatfield, the park keeper, still remembered by many local people for his friendly smile and one eye. His duties included the upkeep of the dovecote, the tennis courts, the putting green and the swing park.

the landing by the staff cloakroom.

'The wash basins near the west door were only constructed after extensive alterations, and in that area we used to be able to look down the old well of the Priory and go into a little cell which had a heavy steel door and a stained-glass window.' (This had been Lady Henry Somerset's private chapel, adapted for use as a strongroom by the Beattys. The stout window grille is still there.)

Mr Claytor ended 'There is a certain magic about the Priory which will always be a part of the place, whoever occupies it.'

He made his own contribution to that magic. Mr Claytor's portrait by Michael Noakes still hangs in the Holbein Hall. For some time he cycled 40 miles each day - 20 miles each way, from Walton-on-Thames. Though he had only one arm he was an able cricketer and had the reputation of wielding the slipper powerfully too. At first, his office was a tiny room overlooking the inner courtyard, but later he moved into the large pleasant room opposite the east end of the Holbein Hall, likely to have been the Lady Chapel of the medieval Priory. This must be the most handsome and historic head teacher's office in Surrey. He was greatly loved and respected, for he established a school where everyone worked together as a team - staff, pupils, clerical and domestic helpers, the park keepers too.

Priory pupils from those earliest Secondary School years still vividly remember their teachers - Mr Angus, Mr Cassingham, Mr Pauer, Mr Burgess, Mrs Nicholls, Mr Torn and others. They all had difficult conditions to contend with, for there was little heating or lighting, and only coke or oil stoves. Workmen were banging away, removing dry rot, installing pipes, replacing floor boards and rewiring, even while lessons were in progress.

The historic chimney piece in the Holbein Hall was still protected by 'a white metal fence', but when Arts Council inspectors viewed the building some time later, they were so impressed by the care shown by pupils and staff, that the barricades were removed.

The ancient Priory bell, recast in 1683, came once more into use, not to call the canons and townspeople to worship, or to warn of fire or invasion, but to call the children to lessons and Assembly. The bell rope was threaded through a hole in the ceiling of the staff room up on the first floor.

At first the old Drawing Room beside the Library became a gymnasium. Lady Henry Somerset's

Dining Room, now with its gold ceiling, was used (horror of horrors!) as a Science lab. But when some wartime huts at Woodhatch became available, Priory pupils walked down Cockshot Hill for woodwork, cookery, needlework and some science lessons. Each year in the summer term Mr Angus and Mr Burgess organised a splendid science exhibition down there.

'The Burgess-Angus close alliance
 Teaches us the laws of Science'
said a rhyme in *Priory News*. Later Mr Cassingham, the patient and gentlemanly craft specialist, supervised the huts, and pupils spent a whole day there instead of going to and fro.

Assemblies of the whole school, such as prize-givings, were often held in the inner courtyard which still had its sundial standing on the little patch of grass. The *Priory News* dated July '49 gives us a glimpse:

'During the recent spell of hot weather the Magnolia buds have burst into full bloom. Their large, white flowers make a glorious splash of colour against the russet brick-work of the Sundial Court wall.

'The appearance of the courtyard has improved tremendously, following the clearance of the builders' rubbish which littered the place in the early days. An attempt has been made to trim the tiny lawn on which the sundial stands, and the whole effect is one of considerable improvement.'

One memorable outdoor occasion was held there in 1953, Coronation Year, when an impressive oak reading desk made by Mr Cassingham was dedicated for use at morning prayers. (This is still used occasionally.)

Each year, every teacher and pupil was marshalled in tiered lines on the grass at the front of the Priory, for the School Photograph. Now, in the '90s, ex-pupils visiting the Museum find great pleasure in running their fingers along the lines of faces, until suddenly they stop - 'There - that's me!'. Then the reminiscences come tumbling out, of the fun and the frights they had, of their old school friends, of the head, the teachers, their nicknames and their idiosyncrasies. Without exception they remember their schooldays here with great pleasure and pride.

The dark and spooky coppice to the east of the Priory was cleared and hard-surfaced in 1953 to create the Bell Street municipal car park. Two years later new buildings were constructed on land to the north, providing a splendid new gymnasium, with

A section of the Priory Secondary School official photograph, taken in October 1950 - boys one side and girls the other. Seated nine places to the left of Mr Claytor, the headmaster, was a young student teacher, Peter Pratt, who was to become Priory head thirty years later.

showers, changing rooms and storerooms attached. The children themselves raised the money for the stage curtains and lighting equipment. The new block included a range of three extra classrooms. One was equipped as a Science Lab and the others for teaching commercial subjects.

Many years later, in the '70s, when the Priory had become a middle school, the facilities were further improved by the addition of cloakrooms and lavatories. When trenches were dug for the foundations we kept a hopeful eye for historic artefacts, but the 'finds' were mainly broken Victorian glass and pottery, bones from the kitchen and old metal fittings - from the days when household rubbish was buried in the garden.

The gardeners' bothy and some of the greenhouse walls, many of them limewashed, survived nearby, until they were cleared in the early '90s for the supermarket development.

Snippets from the *Priory News* make us realise that the Priory School had many facets.

Feb '53. 'David Oram, our Head Boy, tells us that his grandfather, still living, used as a boy to climb up the Priory chimneys to sweep them.'

Feb '53. 'This coming Easter will mark the end of Spurgeon's Homes at Reigate and we will be very sorry to leave the Priory School. (Patrick Bailey)' (This was a Baptist Orphanage which had been evacuated to St David's, Wray Park Road, during the war).

Feb '53. 'From March 1st the price of school dinners will be 9d full cost, 5d half cost. Free dinners will remain the same price!'

Dec '53. 'My grandad, Mr Coomber, worked at the Priory as a gardener for 52 years. He also cut out from two trees the peacocks which are outside room 75 (by the brick path).'

March '58 'We thought a stink bomb had been left in the History room, until we found it was Mr Burgess making a model gas works in the Science room.'

Priory Historians

From the start, the history of the Priory was given a special place in the school's curriculum. The school teams were named Warenne, Augustine, Lymden and Howard, and a school badge was designed, which used the cross of the Knights Hospitallers to suggest the Priory's Augustinian origins. A little rhyme helped the children to remember the sequence of Priory owners:-

'Our founder was Warenne, the sixth earl of Surrey.
The monks of Augustine left here in a hurry.
As sailors and statesmen the Howards are famed.
The Parsons as Lord Mayors of London are named.
Dick Ireland, the grocer, was John Wesley's friend.
The Somers were squires on whom all could depend.
As sailor and horseman Earl Beatty was thorough.
Now the Priory's a school and belongs to the Borough.'

In the school's early days its enthusiastic historian was Mr Boswell. It is apparent that he made both local and general history exciting and amusing. In his large classroom above Lady Henry Somerset's fine dining room, there were displays of artefacts and models he had constructed to illustrate his lessons, along with all sorts of interesting old objects lent by pupils, parents and friends.

Mr Boswell was greatly helped by Ernest Scears, a competent local historian, who was researching the Priory's history with great thoroughness, building on earlier work by Dr Wilfrid Hooper. This exciting research was passed on to the Priory pupils with enthusiasm and skill. He wrote a potted history in serial form for the *Priory News* and illustrated it by his own amusing little drawings.

In 1958, Ernest Scears published a most informative fifty-page booklet, '*A History of Reigate Priory* - with particulars of the notable people who have owned the Priory and lived there, and of the structural alterations carried out by them.' This was a digest of the information which he had systematically stored in a series of black files. Though the booklet is now out of print, the source material is still available for reference at the Priory.

Early in the 1950s another local history enthusiast joined the staff. James Batley, tall and erudite, at once interested himself in the Priory's history and developed a concern for the building which remained for the rest of his life.

Mr Boswell and James Batley were responsible for the Priory School's contribution to *Voices from the Past*, an ambitious exhibition held at the Priory in June 1955. The theme was the history of education in southern Surrey. Fifty schools took part and there were over 2000 visitors.

A film strip about the Priory's history was an extra attraction. For the photographs they borrowed costumes from the Pageant wardrobe and searched out pictures, plans, maps, models, even horses and vehicles from many different sources.

Though James Batley left the Priory soon afterwards, in order to travel round the world, he retained close links, and his interest remained, to be rekindled after the start of our museum nearly twenty years later,.

James Batley came back to the Priory for the last time, only a few days before he died in 1982. He came to dedicate his parting gift, the handsome lantern which now illuminates the grand staircase, replacing Sir John Parsons' sparkling chandelier which disappeared sometime in the 1940s. The enthusiastic 'thank-you letters' from the Priory children made a most moving tribute at Mr Batley's funeral.

The Priory Pageants

There is another aspect of the Priory's history which took place in those post-war years. There were five pageants, each performed over two weeks in September:

1951   A Pageant of Reigate
1953   The Heritage of the Crown
1956   Surrey Cavalcade
1959   Priory Panorama
1963   The Unsheathed Sword

The moving spirit for these great enterprises was Cecile Hummel, a most gifted lady with a powerful personality which could move mountains and command armies. Trained as a Froebel teacher, she came from an acting family with a special interest in historical costume. Miss Hummel is remembered by hundreds of past pupils from her schools at Chipstead and Merstham, and by thousands of people in Reigate and Redhill who took part in or

The Pageant portrayed an imagined event - Queen Elizabeth I arriving in her royal coach to confer upon Charles Howard the title Earl of Nottingham.

Local amateurs from all walks of life took part in the Priory Pageants. In the 1959 programme grateful acknowledgements were made 'to Home Counties Dairies for Pageant publicity on their milk bottle tops'.

watched those Priory Pageants. The whole community, every local organisation, was involved, and they all describe those great events as some of the happiest days of their lives.

The five pageants were enacted in the park, on the vast green arena, between the South Front of the Priory and the wooded greensand ridge. They were always presented in the dark, with dramatic lighting effects. Great stands were erected for the thousands of spectators, and each performance was opened by some personality of note, such as the Lord Mayor of London, Margot Fonteyn or Sybil Thorndike.

The fourth pageant, in September 1959, was *Priory Panorama*. As usual, Cecile Hummel had written the excellent script herself, using Ernest Scears' invaluable black files for her research and conferring with James Batley throughout. The programme carried the names of many people who are still prominent and active in the life of the Borough - some of whom continue to contribute their time and skills to the Priory Museum today. John and Barbara Ferguson merit special mention, for John designed and built scenery, designed the programme and gave his professional advice on heraldry; Barbara worked mainly on costume.

Naturally, *Priory Panorama* finished with a portrayal of the Priory as a school, so Miss Hummel invited the Priory staff and pupils to produce and perform their own scene. This involved them in long hours of evening rehearsals, but it was an unforgettable experience. The *Priory News* reporters wrote 'Best of all was the torchlight procession at the end. We marched into the arena carrying flaming torches, symbols of the torch of learning.'

Throughout the 1950s there was another part of the school's success which was largely attributable to the Priory's location in the park. There were excellent facilities for football, hockey, cricket, netball and athletics which enabled the school to reach very high standards and to win awards in many aspects of sport. A photographic record of Sports Days and other special events was kept by the Science Master, Don Burgess. Together with his large collection of copies of *Priory News*, he most kindly made it available to us for reference.

We are reminded how much we owe to the foresight and energy of Ernest Lancashire, Frank Potter and their supporters, who saved the Priory park for everyone to enjoy, but especially so that young people could use the extensive open space for playing fields.

Reigate Priory County Secondary School for Girls

'Sad News', 'Kiss the Boys Goodbye', 'Petticoat Priory'. The headlines of the 1963 Souvenir Edition of *Priory News* carried the news of a major change for the Priory School. By now large new secondary schools had been built at Redhill and Woodhatch, so the Priory was to become, in stages, a smaller secondary school for girls. Mr Claytor had moved in 1957 and by 1963, Mr Hewett had been the Priory's headmaster for six years. Now he was to become the head of the new Redstone School at

Redhill and Miss Madge Hunt was appointed to be head at the Priory. Sadly, Mr Hewett died in October '65 after only two years in his new post. Miss Hunt moved to be head of the Bishop Simpson School at Redhill, now St Bede's. Mrs Price, who had joined the Priory staff in 1959, was appointed to act as the Priory head for the next few years.

By now the school was working up to 'O' level standard and achieving creditable academic results. There were two memorable dramatic events around this time, both of them instigated by Doris Ker, a highly talented member of the Priory staff, who had earlier experience in writing and publishing. Many of her scripts had been broadcast by the BBC. One of her Priory productions was a witty musical on the suffragette theme, performed with great vivacity by the Priory girls. Male parts were played by imported Grammar School boys.

The second of Doris Ker's outstanding productions was simply entitled *An Evening at Reigate Priory*. This was an ingenious and amusing presentation of the Priory's history, as told by an estate agent showing round prospective buyers in 1921. Characters were portrayed by leading local adult actors, and music from each era was performed on appropriate instruments.

In the early '70s, an unusual situation arose. Mrs Price's husband had been for some years the headmaster of the Holmesdale Primary School (Junior and Infants), less than a mile from the Priory. When Surrey schools were re-organised in 1971, the decision was made to use Reigate Priory as a middle school for children between 8 and 12 years old, and in two phases, to transfer the secondary pupils to other local schools.

The head of this new middle school was to be Clifford Price. So for one year, both Mr and Mrs Price operated as head teachers of the two schools in Reigate Priory.

Reigate Priory Middle School

Only a week or so after we came as a family to live in Reigate in 1959, Cecile Hummel's pageant *Priory Panorama* had introduced me to the Priory, but now, in 1971, my long close association was to begin. I came as a part-time teacher with the first group of Holmesdale children to form the new Middle School.

BBC gardening correspondent Fred Streeter, with head teacher Miss Madge Hunt, presenting prizes at the Priory School Sports Day in 1963. Fred Streeter had been a gardener at the Priory many years earlier.

Clifford Price, a pioneer in audio-visual aids, with an ebullient personality.

Children operated the controls in the CCTV control room, formerly the housemaid's sitting room.

We moved into the Priory in two stages, the ten-year-olds in September 1971 and the rest in '72. Some children came from the Parish School in London Road, but the majority came from Holmesdale School with Clifford Price and many of his staff, leaving the five to seven-year-old children behind at their newly-formed first schools. Both the Holmesdale and Parish schools had traditional Victorian buildings with interesting origins. The Parish School had been founded in 1854 as a National School, for children of Church of England families. The British School for nonconformists had been founded in the High Street in 1852, then moved to its new site in Holmesdale Road in the 1860s.

The school already had its own century of history in Holmesdale Road. Now as a middle school we were moving into a building with a much longer pedigree. We were determined that the excellent teaching tradition, inspired by the Priory itself, must be maintained. But the Priory's new

headmaster brought some unusual educational equipment to assist in this.

At Holmesdale he had established a closed-circuit television studio, housed in a converted playground shelter and equipped with cameras, lighting, sound mixer, monitors and microphones, begged from the BBC and many other sources. All this was adapted to be operated by children, who presented their own programmes and even coped with some of the technical maintenance. This was a 'state of the art' medium with great educational potential. There are many children who owe their successful careers to that project, which stimulated so many different talents.

Teachers discovered that their techniques were sharpened and that the medium was particularly useful when experiments, pictures and objects could be shown. It was a useful tool, particularly in the teaching of science, history, art and craft. Many visitors appeared - some well-known personalities and some with special skills.

Soon the system was installed at the Priory and very soon an appropriate project arose, when County grants were being given to schools, to commission original works of art from local artists. Geoff Miller, a leading Reigate personality, was chosen. He decided to create a large picture of the south front of Reigate Priory, in the form of a lino print. Every stage of the creation of this picture was recorded and shown in our own CCTV studio, from the initial drawing, through the transfer of the image on to lino, then the cutting and finally the printing. This resulted in an excellent and accurate picture, and about twenty prints were taken, but unfortunately the original lino-cut has disappeared. The magic of the zoom lens made it possible for hundreds of children to watch the intricacies of every process on the TV screen in the comfort of their own classrooms.

Newer technology soon brought changes, however. The convenience of the cam-corder and the video cassette made the television studio obsolete. Television was, and still is, a valuable educational tool, but there are drawbacks. One shortcoming is that, however large, the image is second-hand and only two-dimensional.

Meanwhile, the middle school settled in well. Only Doris Ker remained from the earlier staff and everyone else, teachers and children, was new to the building. We had a lot to learn. The Priory's long history, its special atmosphere and its beautiful surroundings gave a certain dignity and helped to

attract high calibre staff. Numbers varied between four and five hundred boys and girls of mixed abilities in classes of different sizes according to the areas available. The old kitchen, the servants' hall and the larger bedrooms made spacious classrooms for 30 children, but smaller rooms such as the old day nursery were a tight fit for 24.

The gold-ceilinged dining room made a perfect music room, now fitted with acoustic panels over walls previously lined with brocade or tapestry. The former servants' hall became a language laboratory with individual booths wired to the latest technology for the teaching of French.

The boot room and the adjoining store-room had been fitted by the Secondary School with a sizeable pottery kiln. When June Keeble, an enthusiastic and gifted new member of staff, took charge, the Middle School children produced remarkable results which were greatly admired in various art and craft exhibitions. Lady Henry Somerset would have been delighted!

The new school was particularly fortunate to

The school gymnasium was purpose-built in 1955. Since then the scope has widened considerably to include school plays, concerts, staff pantomimes, family quizzes, discos, hobby displays, 'frost fairs', talent shows, costume parades and even a planetarium dome.

A pottery class in the old 'boot hole'.

HRH the Princess Anne as she arrived to review the rally of St John Ambulance Cadets at Reigate Priory on June 28th 1980.

inherit so many of the Secondary School facilities. The gymnasium was the best in Surrey. There were two fully fitted home economics rooms, with their own little flat for practising house-keeping skills. The craft room was fitted out with power tools and a brazing hearth.

Most impressive was the handsome Palladian library, created over a century earlier by the third Earl Somers. No leather-bound, gold-tooled books remained, but every shelf was fully stocked with reference and reading matter for children and teachers.

The park, with its lawns and woods, the gardens, the lake and the playing fields continued as a beautiful and healthy setting. The natural environment was there on the doorstep to be enjoyed and studied. In the 1970s the school set up a Nature Trail in the woods - to be shared with other local schools. A special survey was made of the Priory section of the Greensand Way and this won for the school an environmental award.

This sounds like a prospectus for an expensive, privately-run establishment, but Reigate Priory is a particularly fortunate state school. There is more to tell concerning the Priory Museum, the exciting new educational development which was to provide an extra dimension for both the school and the community, but that deserves its own special chapter. First, the story of the Middle School must be brought up to date.

When Cliff Price retired in 1979, the school presented him with, amongst other things, a splendid reel-to-reel video-tape recorder. With it came a video tape, secretly made 'in house', portraying the Priory's history, its architectural features and his last batch of pupils and staff. There could not have been a more appropriate gift for a man who for so many years had promoted audio-visual aids, not only in his own school, but throughout the county.

Peter Pratt, previously headmaster of Furzefield School at Merstham, came to the Priory as head in January 1980, but the Priory was not new to him, for he had spent some time here as a student in 1949. He still has a painful memory of being entrusted with a class to take from the Priory to their Woodhatch outpost and discovering that one boy had been left behind at the 'Angel' crossroads.

On Saturday 28th June 1980, in Peter Pratt's first year as head of the Priory, there was a royal visit. HRH the Princess Anne came to review a rally of St John Ambulance Cadets from Hampshire, Kent, Surrey and Sussex. The review was in the park, just south of the sunken garden, then the Princess had tea and sandwiches in the Priory's gold-ceilinged dining room, where she enjoyed looking at the colourful display of historical pictures specially painted for her by the Priory children. The head-teacher's cloakroom was specially redecorated beforehand.

There were two mementoes of this visit. Peter Pratt received an award, making him an Honorary Member of the St John Ambulance Brigade. The second was a gift to the school of an album of photographs recording this royal occasion.

In 1985 Peter Pratt retired and Mrs Gilly Cox was appointed to be the Priory's new head teacher. The building, the park, and the educational opportunities were to her an exciting prospect.

Her initiation was rather spectacular. Five weeks into her first term, Mr and Mrs Cox attended a glittering banquet in the Holbein Hall. We had organised this jointly through our Priory Museum and the local Heritage Trust, to celebrate, as we thought at the time, the Priory's 750th Anniversary. The real Duke of Norfolk himself presided, as the head of the Howard family. Every guest arrived wearing costume representing a personality associated with the Priory's history. Black canons, bishops, kings, Evelyn, Ussher, Wesley, various Howards (including Admiral Charles), Sir John and Humphrey Parsons, their wives, three Earls Somers, Lady Henry Somerset, Admiral and Countess Beatty and many more!

As the banners, the scrolled menus, the music and the company combined to make an indelible experience, Mrs Cox realised she had taken on a school with a plus and she would be responsible for taking the Priory forward into the future.

A particularly exciting opportunity arose seven years later, in 1992, when Alison Heath, on behalf of Educational Services in Museums, invited Gilly Cox to take 16 Priory children to represent Great Britain in a 'Fête des Enfants d'Europe'. The chosen theme was 'L'Europe des Fleuves' and each team was to prepare an imaginative presentation portraying their nearest river. So the Priory children explored every aspect of the River Mole, which they expressed in music and poetry, film, photographs, even a massive physical map in plaster.

The children and the displays were packed into the school mini-bus, with the huge plaster map strapped on top. An odd corner was found for a few balls and other sports equipment.

Two thousand school children met at the Château Scéaux near Paris, each team wearing a coloured scarf to indicate their country of origin. In spare moments, out came the footballs, everyone joined in and the 'togetherness' overcame all barriers.

There have been Priory links with Europe throughout the centuries - Prior John Lymden, William and Charles Howard, John and Humphrey Parsons, the third Earl Somers and Admiral Beatty often crossed the Channel. The 20th Century Priory schoolchildren went chiefly to promote international understanding.

There has been rapid change in the world of education since Gilly Cox became head of the Priory. Even the tools for education have changed and the development of information technology demands a computer for every class and even the school's own computer suite.

In 1988 came a new Education Act, which led to the National Curriculum and a great emphasis on assessment and evaluation, creating more paper-work for teachers. From 1990, Local Management for Schools put a heavy burden of responsibility on school governors and heads.

Reigate Priory School

In 1993, Middle Schools for 8 - 12 year-olds in Surrey came to an end and the school at the Priory became a Junior School for children aged 7 to 11, but it was to be known just as Reigate Priory School. There were no dramatic changes, only lower furniture for the youngest children and a slight shift in the curriculum.

The ethos of the school remains the same. Gilly Cox places top priority on respect at all levels, on character development and self-discipline. The educational programme is highly stimulating, to give children both intellectual and physical challenge. As well as the Priory-based programme,

Mrs Gilly Cox, the head teacher of Reigate Priory School since 1985.

there are residential visits, which every child has a chance to attend. Climbing, camping, language study and ski-ing in France, mountain walking in Wales and many more activities are on the menu, and as the children build up their confidence and self-esteem, these are reflected in their academic achievement.

Fun comes high on the agenda, with great input from the staff and the Parent Teacher Association. Every year there is a fête - with a theme - The Wild West, Space, Tropical Islands - when everyone dresses up. Mrs Cox is always the life and soul of the party, usually wearing her favourite colour - purple. The figure of Don Holman the former caretaker will long be remembered as Father Christmas, Henry VIII or, for more formal occasions, the Priory butler. Firework displays, splendid musical and dramatic productions - all add to the fun and often the funds too.

Every seven-year-old in 'Year 3' starts with a friend at the Priory already, for Noel Lellman, year leader and a deputy head, will have visited the contributing schools beforehand, to make a link with every child and family. In their first week or two, it is Noel Lellman who shows them the geography of the building, the assembly hall, Mrs Cox's room and the office, the toilets - the Priory they are using today.

Gradually, the children begin to realise that the Priory is more than a school, it is a very old building which has been lived in and worked in, by all sorts of people, for eight hundred years.

Over the next few months, Noel Lellman takes them on a similar tour, but back in time 700 years or more, to the nave of the Priory church, to the Lady Chapel, the north porch and the bell tower. Outside, the likely location of the cloisters, the garth, the dormitory, refectory and Prior's lodging are described and imagined. The really important questions are answered too - 'Are there any skeletons?' - 'Where were the toilets and what were they like?'.

At this stage, for several years, came the traditional test of ingenuity for every Priory pupil and parent. They were asked to create, at home, a model of a Black Canon, preferably with moveable eyes and limbs (History and Design Technology combined here!). I am sure that more Black Canons have been created by Priory School children over the years, than ever lived here over earlier centuries.

Some weeks later, the time tour takes the children to the same starting place, but only 450 years back, to imagine it as the Great Hall of a Tudor mansion, with the Howard coat of arms newly painted on the stone fireplace arch. Overhead, a fine plaster ceiling has been constructed and the ancient stone walls are covered by panelling and tapestries, except on the south side where the sun makes new patterns as it shines through stone mullioned windows and there is a delightful view of the deer herd in the park and the wooded hills beyond. The cloisters and the refectory have gone, but the foundations remain below the grass. On the pediment, high on the South Front, they pick out the royal coat of arms, which the famous Lord High Admiral was specially permitted to place there in honour of the great Queen Elizabeth I.

Back in a classroom on the north side of the courtyard, the young Charles Howard is conjured up, swishing his racquet and thwacking hard balls against the wall, in a fast game of Royal Tennis (The language of hazards and chases is **not** in the syllabus). This was, almost certainly, the location

'Awesome!' The children are deeply impressed by the pediment. If Charles Howard had displayed the royal coat of arms without Elizabeth's consent, he could have lost his head.

An exercise in investigating the Priory's history by observing and recording the details of the south front.

of the Tennis House at Reigate Priory but, as we know, it was burned down in 1575.

Perhaps the favourite step back in time takes the children to Lady Henry Somerset's Priory, only a century ago. The classrooms upstairs become bedrooms again, with canopied beds and fine French furniture. The children visit the old nurseries in the south-east corner and love to hear the stories about the rebellious little Isabel.

History to the Priory children is about real people, who actually lived here. Their time sense develops early and dates become pegs on which to hang more knowledge. Not only does the building have a story to tell, it arouses an interest in art, architecture and craftsmanship.

The walls and corridors of the Priory are bright with pictures and displays related to many topics, but there is one painted on the wall of the long ground floor corridor, at child's eye level, which is especially valuable. It is a pictorial time-line setting the Priory's 800 years of history in context.

The Priory children appreciate their building, they respect it and are proud of it. They learn to know and understand their immediate environment. This seems to enrich their lives today, for the school hums with activity and the children are happy, enthusiastic, polite and considerate.

For most of us, our view of the Priory School as we walk through the Priory park, is rather like a Lowry picture brought to life in the hundreds of little stick figures walking, running, jumping and skipping in the playground, on both sides of the Eagle Gateway. In their red sweatshirts or grey pullovers with the ancient building for a backdrop, it is rather a beautiful picture.

But an important chunk of the Priory's history is still to be told.

It concerns the most recent development and will, we trust, take the story of Reigate Priory far into the future.

The 'Peacock Door' on the east side of the building is now the official main entrance. The Great West Door was the Priory's original entrance, and was in use for nearly five hundred years, until Sir John Parsons created the portico on the south front c. 1700. From 1893, Lady Henry Somerset used the Courtyard Door on the north side of the main building.

REIGATE PRIORY MUSEUM

So Reigate Priory has played a variety of rôles, as a religious house, as a country home for a succession of important families, as a safe haven for wartime offices, and now as a state school, but a school with an extra dimension - the museum.

Now, in 1998, Reigate Priory Museum has been running for twenty-five years but, as we look back, we realise that the ground was being prepared much earlier. The painstaking research by Dr Hooper and Ernest Scears; the caring concern for both the Priory building and the park by Mr Potter, Mr Lancashire and more recently by James Batley; the enthusiasm and interest shown by Mr Boswell and then a succession of teachers at the Priory - all these were making their contribution.

My own part in the story began when we came as a family to live in Reigate in 1959. First came the pageant, *Priory Panorama*. Then, ten years of part-time teaching at Holmesdale School proved to be invaluable, for as a newcomer to Reigate I was learning alongside the children. There was so much to discover here. Starting from the street names - Holmesdale Road, Warren Road, Wray Common, Somers Road, Rushworth Road, we built up our knowledge of the town and its history, its geology, its buildings and its people.

We went out to explore. We visited the Holmesdale Natural History Club's Museum on our doorstep, the Cranston Library in the Parish Church, and many private collections. As we questioned people with vivid memories of old Reigate - Walter Bushby, Geoff Miller, Flossie Willard, Eric Hurst, Olive Holmes and many more - Victorian and Edwardian Reigate came alive in the classroom. Interestingly, the Priory had played a part in all their lives.

Soon the classroom became a mini-museum, with its samples of sand, chalk, Reigate stone and clay, locally made pots, Frith pictures of old Reigate, newspapers and even a Reigate fireman's brass helmet.

The opportunity

In 1970, when Clifford Price, Holmesdale's head teacher, was appointed to be head at Reigate Priory, he realised that the building brought not only new responsibilities, but also unique opportunities. Its history, its architecture and its setting would give the school a new dimension.

However, some rooms could not be used as classrooms, being too large, too small or having problems of access. In discussion, we saw an opportunity to create an exciting educational resource - the Priory's own museum. This could be of great value, not only to the Priory children but to all schools, both state and private. It could be a community project and a community resource which would interest visitors to the Borough too.

The vision - a new kind of museum

At that time the word 'museum' suggested a dim, quiet, old building full of dusty glass cases with fading labels - certainly not the image to fit our vision.

Visits to museums all over the country helped in the planning of a museum which would meet our special needs, but no prototype existed, for our circumstances and our ideals were unique.

Since that time thirty years ago, most museums have become places of active, exciting discovery. There were stirrings of change in some of the more enterprising museums in London, such as the Geffrye Museum and the Horniman Museum,

Priory exhibitions have scope for activity and involvement.

Reproduced by kind permission of the Croydon Advertiser Group.

borrowed from the Borough and County archives. A separate display showed the more general sort of material we wished to acquire, mainly from local sources, to enable us to present changing exhibitions.

At that time a Surrey Museums Committee was being set up, to link professional curators from the local authority museums with amateurs like myself, from independent museums. These meetings were most encouraging and helpful, for the professionals gave generous moral and practical support and the day courses provided training in many useful skills. One useful skill I had was in simple calligraphy, which came in very handy for making legible labels.

It was astonishing to find at least a dozen local museums and collections in our own borough. One or two, like the Holmesdale Natural History Club's museum in Croydon Road, and the museum of mental health at the Royal Earlswood Hospital were occasionally open to the public. Some of the collections, like the TUC's national collection of Trade Union material, crammed into a house in Cornfield Road, or the little museum at the Crusader Insurance Company's head office at Woodhatch, were quite unknown to the public. There were other collections, such as Ian West's collection of North American Indian Art and Miss Clements' costume collection, whose owners were longing to have an opportunity to display their treasures.

All these were keen to support our new venture and to lend exhibits.

where Alison Heath and Dr Elizabeth Goodhew were establishing busy education departments. These were making a startling impact for they were involving people from all backgrounds in a wide variety of museum-based activities, not only academic, but some very practical. Art, crafts, music, dancing, acting and scientific experiments made the museums more alive and meaningful.

Support and interest

From the very beginning we realised that we needed advice and support. So we invited to the Priory many of Surrey's historians, County and Borough officials, representatives from other museums and from local organisations.

We presented a double bill - a repeat performance of *An Evening at Reigate Priory* and a display of Priory-related material - much of it

Establishing the Collection

Soon we discovered that there was a wealth of material hidden away in desks and drawers, in cellars and in attics. Many elderly people were delighted to learn that the information they had saved could be preserved and displayed for others to enjoy.

Walter Bushby cleared his attic to start us off with a wonderful array of local and domestic memorabilia, and he did not stop there. In his 90s, he made and gave to us typescripts of his memories and of the mass of local history material he had built up during his long life in Reigate.

We wrote to the *Times, Country Life* and other national publications alerting readers to our hunt for Priory-related artefacts and information. Very soon, these enquiries resulted in James Batley's find - the missing portrait of John Lymden, Reigate's last

The Museum has built up a large collection of domestic bygones, discarded by local people when clearing their attics and cellars.

Prior. This was the first of many new discoveries, all of them bringing us closer to the people who have created the Priory's story.

From the very beginning our local newspapers took a great interest in the Museum project and gave generous publicity. In 1985 the *Surrey Mirror* published a special illustrated issue which stimulated local people to send in their own memories.

The Priory families thoroughly enjoyed collecting objects with interesting local connections. One child brought a huge ammonite found on Reigate Hill during the construction of the motorway. Another brought a lantern used in Victorian days for showing people round the Reigate caves. There were medallions struck in 1863 when Reigate became a Borough and a tiny pair of shoes made by a Reigate shoemaker for his own little daughter.

However, enthusiasm had to be curbed at times. One little boy offered to climb over the handrail and get the large Borough badge from the bridge over Reigate Hill. Two children contributed the skeleton of a cat, which made a fascinating puzzle and kept them busy for hours identifying the pieces using a diagram from a book in the library.

The children gathered local information too. During the Easter holiday of 1972, every Priory child found someone who had lived in Reigate for 40 years or more. They recorded memories of schooldays, events, shops, transport, health, food and clothes, either in written form, or on tape. Some firm friendships were made, and many of the children brought these older friends regularly to the museum in later years.

A hoard of Victorian and Edwardian clothing and accessories established the Museum's costume collection, which is now one of the most important in the county. This gift came from Mrs Bobbie Wilkins, who was a school manager at the time. For 20 years she used her influence to promote the Museum whenever possible, and when the Museum Committee was formed in 1992 she was the obvious chairman. Very sadly she died suddenly in 1994 but her enthusiasm is now maintained by her husband.

The official opening

By February 1973 we were ready for an official opening. For this occasion we invited Derek Bilton, who had set up an innovative Museum Loan Service for schools in Nottinghamshire. His title, *The Magic of Museums* drew a packed audience in the Priory's Holbein Hall. First, as one might expect, he showed slides, pictures of great works of art and of puzzling objects for us to identify. Next he passed around actual things - fossils and flints, pottery and coins, a Victorian toy, a ration book and a gas mask.

There were smells too, in bags and bottles - Lifebuoy soap, paraffin, soot and camphor. Other smells were unpleasant and unfamiliar. The scent of fox, badger and fungus made us quickly replace the caps on the bottles. Next came sounds - a wartime siren and a gas rattle, a steam train, bird song, clogs on cobbles. Last came tastes and textures, tried on blindfolded volunteers - syrup of figs, tripe and pear-drops.

His message was clear. A good museum should stimulate our memory, our curiosity and our

imagination. It will inform us through all our senses. It will enrich our knowledge and understanding, but best of all, it will fill us with wonder.

We could not have wished for a more inspiring launch.

Welcome to the Museum

The Museum was now officially open for the public as well as for school use. A 'handy' father constructed a signboard and a Museum logo was designed by another parent - symbolising our collections of Local History (the Priory crosses) and childhood - or Victoriana (the rocking horse).

Museum visitors use either the South or the East Door, which is known as the Peacock Door, for the topiary birds are quite recognisable now. (In *Priory News*, July 1952 there was an amusing item:- **'Peacock hatches chicks**. Few people know that in one of our ornamental peacocks not more than three yards from the Main Entrance a thrush decided to build a nest and hatch four sturdy youngsters').

As they walk through the main hall, visitors stop to admire the Howard fireplace, the Holbein overmantel and John Parsons' grand staircase. Some, especially children, notice the huge glass case full of exotic stuffed birds, and they either love it or hate it. Recently, we made a discovery at the Town Hall. We were shown an album full of late Victorian photographs of Woodhatch House, the property designed by Michael Searles (whom we have met already as the architect employed in 1802 by George Mowbray to submit plans for the Priory's west front). Woodhatch House was pulled down in the 1960s and replaced by houses in Lime Close, but the contents had been sold many years earlier. Standing on the landing, shown in one photograph, were two glass cases, full of stuffed birds, and one of these is clearly recognisable. It was purchased by a local resident at the clearance sale and a hunt through the copies of *Priory News* reveals that it was generously presented to the school by Mr and Mrs Fleming in 1955.

Sometimes, conducted tours of the building start from the Holbein Hall, and for many years this was the pitch for the Museum Shop. Now the shop is in the Museum, selling Priory-related postcards, tea-towels, books, information packs, with inexpensive pencils, rubbers and badges which children love to buy as souvenirs.

The Museum has always been in the South West corner of the Priory building. At first, we had joint use of the Library, where we mounted changing displays, sometimes spreading into part of an adjoining classroom, the old Drawing Room. At first, our plan was to display costume and Victoriana in the room above, but the fire authorities banned its use by the public, so it became our main storeroom, with extra storage space in the attic. A year or so later the whole of the Drawing Room became available for Museum use, and this happy arrangement remained for many years. In the early 1990s the majestic Palladian library was completely refurbished specifically for Museum use and now this is where every exhibition is held.

Changing exhibitions

A lively museum must have changing displays, and at first they changed in quick succession, as new gifts and loans came along. In the first year, 1973-4, there were eleven -

1. A display of historic equipment given by the Crusader Insurance Company - dictaphone, adding machines, and many other things that worked.
2. Aerial photographs of Reigate lent by Malcolm Pendrill, a well-known local photographer - Spot your own home!
3. Railways - a display presented by four 12-year-old boys, with help from Brockham Railway Museum.
4. World War II - exhibits brought by the children.
5. Images of Reigate - paintings, photographs, maps and models lent by local societies.
6. Canals - help from the Wey and Arun Canal Trust and a display of canal art by a local art student.
7. An exhibition for Queen Victoria's birthday - pictures, costumes, china etc.
8. *Here comes the Bride* (to link with the marriage of Princess Anne) - a display of 40 beautiful wedding dresses - from Victorian to more recent ones lent by parents and Priory staff. Bouquets in correct period style were supplied by a local florist.

9. A display of Surrey Museums loan material, with our own recent acquisitions.
10. *Workmen's tools* - some donated collections and a collection lent and demonstrated by Mr Aldred, the Parks Superintendent.
11. A 150th anniversary exhibition set up by the RNLI - with a real lifeboat (inflatable sections) which took up almost the whole room and which children and adult visitors could climb into and imagine themselves as lifeboatmen or rescued passengers.

The second year was just as exciting and varied, but we began to find that the duration of each exhibition did not give enough time for all the schools and groups who wanted to come. So gradually, we extended them to last for a term. Now the Museum is so well used that they have to last for a year - though sometimes with alterations to the content. For special Saturday events there are extra displays in the entrance hall or in the Holbein Hall.

How did we choose the themes?

The Museum and TV

Other exhibitions were planned to run alongside popular schools TV programmes such as *How we used to live*. Using our rapidly growing collection of historical domestic artefacts, we presented *Upstairs, Downstairs, Exploring Granny's Attic, Rescued from the Past* and others on World War II. Thames TV showed great interest in what we were doing and in 1974 made two of their schools programmes at the Priory, under the titles *Hunting for Clues* and *Digging Around*. Some of our Priory children and some of our adult supporters had starring rôles. We were particularly pleased that these programmes featured the Priory building and showed how we investigated local history. My own vivid memory is of a massive lunch at a local hotel as a guest of the TV crew, wearing a tight Victorian dress and a cumbersome radio microphone. This TV series was very successful and our episodes were repeated for many years.

Local collections

Sometimes a collector or an organisation offered to present an exhibition for us. The local Fire Service, the Redhill Philatelic Club, Warnes the publishers of Beatrix Potter's books all mounted their own exhibitions. Ray Hounslow set up his Post Office

In 1974 copies of this poster were sent by Thames TV to every Junior school in the country.

memorabilia and students from the local school of Art presented an excellent display of Heraldry. All these exhibitions were colourful, clearly understandable, with scope for involvement and for 'hands on' activities, with suitable content and information to interest adults and children alike.

Anniversaries and events

In 1976 we celebrated the five hundredth anniversary of printing in England. (Caxton set up his wooden printing press in Westminster Abbey in 1476). The Reigate School of Art, the *Surrey Mirror* and various printing firms were very helpful, and we were able to give opportunities for all visitors, whatever age, to try some of the processes.

In 1977 came the Royal Silver Jubilee. We drew attention to all the Priory's royal connections, we displayed royal memorabilia and we even borrowed a large portrait of Edward VII, who really did sleep here! from Windsor Castle.

The 17th century broken basin found hidden in the wall - a Priory mystery.

Another commemoration was organised jointly with the local Heritage Trust. 1981 was the centenary of the death of the famous local artist, Samuel Palmer. Though his pictures would not normally be expected to appeal to children, we took up the challenge and it worked. One of his descendants even lent to us a few original paintings and etchings - and a local firm generously insured them for us. We set up Palmer's easel with his usual snack of eggs and apples; we showed scenes from his life - and the children were captured by the magic of his genius.

1985 was - we thought during that year - the year to celebrate the 750th anniversary of the founding of the Priory, but Roger Ellaby, a local researcher, came across new evidence to show that the Priory is older still, so we were in fact a few years late. We had, of course, a superb wrap-around exhibit - the Priory building itself. We displayed our growing collection of authentic artefacts - John Lymden's portrait, the cross piece from the stone mullioned window, Richard Ireland's Priory survey, the broken basin which had been hidden in the wall, the Priory Visitors' Book, Lady Henry Somerset's altar figure and her beautifully illustrated children's book. But to re-create the Priory's past, considerable ingenuity was required. We built the vanished cloisters quite convincingly from cardboard carpet rolls disguised as pillars.

A team of children, guided by a member of the Embroiderers' Guild, made a set of large, brightly coloured banners, representing the badges of the eight main owners of the Priory, and they looked splendid, suspended high above the displays. There were child-sized costumes for the children to put on, to act out a chapter meeting or some other episode from the Priory's history. As always, we organised quizzes, the writing of poems and plays, and drawing sessions outside and inside the building. We planned a programme of special events, including an Adult Education Saturday Seminar when eminent speakers lectured on different aspects of the Priory's history.

In 1988 we celebrated the 400th anniversary of Charles Howard's defeat of the Spanish Armada, with a real 'spectacular'. Two local professional artists, Vera and Ray Strank, offered to help us and so lifted our displays into a higher league. For our commemorative exhibition, *Reigate's Lord High Admiral*, they produced a superb representation of Charles Howard on the deck of his flagship the *Ark Royal*. Stewart Love painted the seascape background. The whole scene was meticulously researched and splendidly painted.

Margaret Watson, who specialises in making replicas of historical costume, dressed figures to represent Queen Elizabeth I, also Charles Howard in his younger days as her Chamberlain of the Royal Household. There were smells too - as Chamberlain, Charles Howard would have been responsible for obtaining exotic herbs and spices from the New World - ours were supplied by a local health-food shop.

Beautiful replicas of sackbuts, serpents and other Elizabethan instruments were lent to us by a world-famous maker who happened to live in Surrey, and we held two or three concerts of music from that period, played on similar replicas. On one memorable Saturday, a society specialising in historic dance, all in authentic costume, presented a display and then invited the audience to join in. To see the Mayor and Mayoress, Cllrs Eddie and Mary Waller, with about 200 other citizens holding joined hands high, dancing out into the grounds, around the sunken garden and back, accompanied by pipe, tabor and other instruments, was a glorious sight.

As we have mentioned, we had some very special guests - Miles Howard,

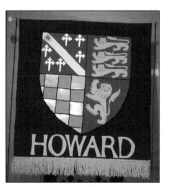

The third in the set of eight heraldic banners.

The Earl and Countess of Effingham meet Queen Elizabeth I and Charles Howard in the Armada Exhibition.

the Duke of Norfolk, returned to open the exhibition and suggested that we should invite his cousin Mowbray Howard, the Earl of Effingham, who, with the Countess, visited the exhibition and mingled with a motley crowd of Elizabethan children (Priory pupils).

Soon afterwards, Vera and Ray Strank expressed their wish to help us again. What about *Alice in Wonderland* in 1990, to celebrate its first publication 125 years earlier, in 1865? We were daunted, for we had no ready-made exhibits - only copies of the book. But Charles Dodgson (Lewis Carroll) knew the Somers family well and probably visited them at the Priory. The children loved the idea, the work team was willing to have a go - so we accepted the challenge. The Stranks offered to create the 'Wonderland' and we provided the educational and academic content for Lewis Carroll's *Alice*.

A parent, Ray Luff, offered to help with the research and to do all the necessary photography. As an employee of British Rail, he was able to travel all over the country taking pictures of *Alice* connections - a unique piece of research now held by the Lewis Carroll Society. He went with us to Christchurch, Oxford, to visit our friend John Norsworthy, who had, when living near Duxhurst, collaborated in a symposium on Lady Henry Somerset. At Oxford he was working closely with the Dean. We had the freedom of the Deanery, where Alice Liddell, the real *Alice*, lived, and the Deanery garden, where Charles Dodgson first saw Alice and her sisters playing. The Librarian unlocked the cupboard of *Alice* and Carroll

treasures and left us to investigate. That was just the beginning.

Vera and Ray Strank reached new heights in producing the Wonderland section of the exhibition, complete with a rabbit hole, the caterpillar sitting on the toadstool smoking his hookah and, wonder of wonders, the Cheshire Cat, appearing and disappearing. Our museum team set up a re-creation of Lewis Carroll's study, with his William de Morgan tiles (cardboard squares, indistinguishable from the originals, painted for us by Sally Dymott, a Priory parent), copies of the very books he owned on the bookshelves, his toy bat (twinkle, twinkle...), a tea-tray set for Alice and her sisters, first editions of his *Alice* books, his actual photograph of Alice - and prints of many of his other photographs, including two of Isabel Somers. The real Alice's grand-daughter, Mary Jean St Clair, came specially to open the exhibition and lent to us, for display, a dress worn by her famous grandmother.

The Museum and Reigate

Everyone enjoys exhibitions about Reigate. For one of these, in 1984, every Priory pupil (considerably helped by skilful parents) made a model of one of the buildings in central Reigate - based on a shoe-box, to ensure a uniform scale. These superb creations, complete with miniature books and newspapers, 'Play-dough' fruit and vegetables, loaves and cakes, shoes, etc. were works of art. The centre-piece was a scale model of the Old Town Hall, made by the models unit of the Department of the Environment. We placed the children's models, at eye level, in order, along our reduced versions of High Street, Church Street and Bell Street. Reigate's architecture and aspects of its history were shown in pictures and models around the walls. Local shopkeepers and businessmen flocked in and later, some of the models were displayed in the premises they had portrayed in miniature.

Over the years many people have given or loaned to the Museum objects with local origins or connections. The largest is a perfect scale model of the Reigate Heath windmill, in wood, standing about four feet high with even longer sweeps. The story of its origins is magical, but too long to be told here. Another is a beautiful model of the Reigate coach which plied between Reigate, Guildford and Southampton.

Priory supporters, parents and children are keen

collectors. One father rescued for us the huge sign which hung outside 'The Old Wheel' in Church Street - a tea and luncheon house of almost sacred memory. Mark Davison of the *Surrey Mirror* rescued the 'White Hart' sign for us only recently.

Exhibitions for people with special interests

Each exhibition drew - besides the children and visiting schools - not only our faithful, regular visitors, but different types according to the subject. *For Workmen's Tools* labourers from a nearby building site popped in during their tea-break. Costume exhibitions were most interesting to ladies. *Trains, planes, cars and buses* (1983, with a real 1902 French car in the Museum), *Stamps* (1974), *Postal History* and *The Story of Printing* (both in 1987) attracted chiefly the men and the boys.

The noisiest exhibitions were two very popular displays of musical instruments, largely organised for us by the writer and artist Lilla Fox, who also designed many of our posters. Some exhibits were very precious or delicate, so we evolved a simple code which worked very well - green labels for the touchables and red labels for those which must not be touched - the 'untouchables'.

We were fortunate in having personalities, people with unique experiences, or people with special skills, who spent hours in the museum sharing their special-ness with visitors, whether adults or children. Deborah Grant the actress, who was also a Priory parent, demonstrated theatrical make-up on the children, and sometimes even her juggling skills when she came in each week to our exhibition *Back Stage*. Roger Mintey described to us in vivid detail, how he found the great Reigate Hoard of coins in September 1990. A picture I shall always carry in my mind is of John Ferguson, an artist of world repute, quietly painting a heraldic badge amid the bustle of the busy museum. A small boy stood watching every brush stroke for a very long time, then went away. But he came back again, touched John to attract his attention and said 'I like painting too!'.

There have been many magic moments - one was when another little boy picked up a fossil, estimated to be 60 million years old. He held it and felt it for a long time, then he said 'That is history, lots and lots and lots of it'. A very moving moment was when Yolande Clements, just 80 years old, saw the exhibition we had prepared in her honour, *All in a Lifetime*. She was speechless as she looked around

The re-creation of Lewis Carroll's study, complete with William de Morgan tiles in replica.

Reigate treasure - Roger Mintey generously gave a selection from this find to the Priory Museum.

Yo Clements (right), aged 80, enjoying our recreation of 'Isola', her popular tea shop in Reigate High Street.

and saw our displays about her childhood in Lincoln early this century, her training as a 'Cordon Bleu' cook, and her Ambulance Service experiences in World War II. Best of all she liked our mock-up of her café 'Isola' which was a popular venue in Reigate's High Street. We had managed to unearth some of her tablecloths and china and a cooker of the right vintage. A parent made cakes each week to be consumed by visitors, helpers and children just before the exhibition closed. Yo was a great collector of costume, cookery books, accessories and crafts, and when she died in 1994 she left most of her vast collection to the Museum.

A success - and a failure

Everyone has a different favourite - my grandchildren loved *Creepy Crawlies* when I had to take some of the living creatures home each night. The giant tortoises from Gatwick Zoo burrowed and escaped from our garden regularly and at the Priory the crickets got into the caretaker's kitchen on the top floor. The snails got out of their tanks and devoured anything green - labels, illustrations, the lot! In the old Drawing Room a local firm fixed a 12 foot square pond, with a waterfall, a fountain, fish, frogs and newts. Giant stick insects kept us all busy providing suitable leaves. On open days the Priory children brought along their guinea pigs, rabbits, hamsters and mice - we had a wonderful time and learned some very interesting things about the habits of creepy crawlies.

Only one exhibition failed to catch on - a hired exhibition about baskets - *The Useful Willow*. We had no opportunity for involvement and it had no 'spark'! From our opening in 1973 to my retirement in 1992 we presented at least fifty exhibitions, and many of the themes were chosen by the Priory children themselves.

Museum visitors

On Wednesdays the Museum is often packed with visiting school parties. Introductory talks and quizzes are available, but most important is the involvement, the close experience. As the space available is only 48' by 24' the children are divided into groups. While one group of children is in the museum, another group may be shown a relevant film or videotape in the hall and another may have a session handling artefacts. The exhibitions are enjoyed by all ages and some topics have appeal for adults with specialist interests. Historical societies, adult education groups, U3A and Townswomen's Guilds have made frequent visits over the years. The Spanish Society, the Oxford Society, a group of London architects, the Surrey Museums Group and many others have visited on occasion.

But it is especially satisfying to see little groups of elderly people meeting in the museum to enjoy reminiscing over the pictures of old Reigate, or to see Priory children proudly bringing parents or grandparents to see their own special Museum.

Museum therapy

A small museum has a lot to offer to people with disabilities. We have usually arranged for such groups to come when the museum is not busy.

Exploring Granny's Attic, a visiting group of children try on the hats.

People with impaired sight, hearing or understanding can enjoy handling some exhibits or trying on certain costumes. For some years, many blind people were able to 'visit' the museum in imagination. Whenever a new exhibition opened, we recorded a 'talk through', complete with sound effects, with the Tandridge Talking Newspaper. This proved very popular with the listeners.

One Wednesday in 1988 a very depressed lady was wheeled in, with her head bowed, with no interest in the brilliant Armada exhibition. She ignored our welcome, so I picked up a handful of dried cloves and asked her what they reminded her of. She sniffed, lifted her head, opened her eyes and smiled. 'Toothache and apple pies, when I was a little girl', she said. Now her interest was aroused, and soon she was enjoying the whole exhibition.

Another rewarding occasion was at Dungate Manor, where I regularly took children to show the residents some of our Museum treasures. One elderly man was very bent and weary, but when we put a curly-brimmed top hat on his head and a cane in his hand, he perked up saucily and regaled us with a music-hall song. Hats work wonders, for people forget themselves and enjoy acting a new part. Strategically placed mirrors come in useful.

The value of reminiscence therapy is now well recognised. Children benefit from the Museum's therapeutic effect too. Bright children are stretched, children with learning problems are stimulated. Children with social problems often find that the museum is a peaceful haven. One large, disruptive boy enjoyed helping to construct our exhibitions and while working near the main staircase he noticed the different marquetry patterns on the stair ends. When we gave him cut-outs of wood-grained Fablon and suggested he might copy the designs, he became completely fascinated and very skilful. Many years later he returned with his wife and family, looking happy and prosperous, to say thank-you. He is now a dealer in antique furniture.

Museum studies on the timetable

All the Priory children are very proud of the Priory building, with its long and varied history. They are very proud too of their own Museum, and of the fact that, as far as we know, theirs is the only school to have Museum Studies on the regular weekly timetable. It is unique. From the beginning the children have found special delight in this privilege, for there is great satisfaction in seeing, touching and investigating real things. Subjects on the National Curriculum are enhanced, and other topics widen their experience.

For about fifteen years this museum-based teaching was my special rôle. More recently Emma Currow, and now Christina Manners, have taught Priory classes in the Museum each morning. Few small museums are so intensively used and no museum could be more enjoyed.

Since the Museum began there has always been a full-time member of the Priory staff responsible for liaison with the Museum and there is, of course, co-operation with class teachers.

Emma Currow taking a group for museum studies.

The Museum has yet another function. It operates a loan service for Priory teachers and for teachers from other schools. This means that some artefacts can be used for normal classroom teaching.

As a bonus, for children who have a very special interest in the Museum, there is the museum club after school. This has provided an opportunity for going out to explore the town's historical buildings, for investigating the museum collection in more depth or for inviting experts to come in to talk about their specialisms or to show their treasures. The children have helped with preparing exhibitions, or with cleaning the less vulnerable artefacts.

Alarming incidents

There have been a few alarming experiences.

One lunch-time early in 1981, someone reported 'smoke' billowing underneath the door of the locked storeroom, just off the landing above the main staircase. Peter Pratt, the headmaster at that time, obtained a key and opened the door, to find the room filled with steam. Very hot water was gushing from a fractured radiator. This happened just after a Christmas holiday of freezing weather. By now, the water was pouring out onto the landing and dripping down into the Holbein Hall. So every member of staff was summoned, with some of the older children, and every available bucket, bowl and tin bath was put to use. A human chain transferred everything movable from the storeroom to the attic, and, miraculously, the only things damaged were cardboard boxes. Their contents were rescued just in time.

Another incident occurred on a Saturday when the Museum was full of visitors. The exhibition was a display of many different arts and crafts and we had arranged a number of demonstrations. The blacksmith was lighting up his portable furnace quite safely out in the courtyard, when the Priory fire-alarms almost split our ear-drums. As the Museum was evacuated, the fire engines raced through the town and to the Priory grounds. The whole building was searched, but there was no fire. The smoke from the blacksmith's furnace had drifted in through open windows and set off the smoke alarms. Our younger visitors found all this rather thrilling, but we felt more than a little embarrassed.

The third incident still makes me shudder. When Ed Stonard took over as Museum Store Manager in 1990 he carefully checked every shelf and cupboard. In one cardboard box he found a collection of wartime relics - fragments of bombs, bits of aircraft, parts of parachutes and so on. Amongst all these was a 'butterfly bomb' given to us by an official expert, with every assurance that it was completely inactive and safe. This rang a bell in Mr Stonard's memory, for he knew that when Prince Charles had a similar bomb in his little collection of interesting items, some knowledgeable person had warned him it was potentially lethal. Apparently bombs of this type cannot be de-activated.

So Ed phoned the Fire Station for advice. They ordered the immediate complete evacuation of the Priory, and fortunately, at first, the children thought it was a routine fire drill. Bomb disposal experts were summoned from Aldershot and given an escort along the M25 and down the hill to the Priory. A hole was dug far out in the Priory field, and the bomb was detonated. They told us it was powerful enough to have destroyed the whole west wing of the Priory. The children were quite safe and enjoyed every moment of the drama, not appreciating the horror of what could have happened. But the classes who had been out on a school visit were quite upset to have missed all the excitement!

The people who make the Museum possible

At Reigate Priory it is vital that the head teacher believes whole-heartedly in the value of the Museum, enjoys being involved, is willing to make space available and to give full backing. The Museum, of course, does all it can to respond to the needs of the school. Fortunately all the Priory school heads, Cliff Price, Peter Pratt and Gilly Cox, have appreciated the Museums's unique contribution to the school and the community.

Since Gilly Cox became head in 1985 she has constantly fought for the conservation of the Priory building and for the best interests of the school and the museum. She joins in the museum planning, in the fun of the museum events and in the excitement of our historical activities. Gilly Cox's influence, with her shared ethos and vision, has steered the museum through many a bureaucratic challenge.

The Borough too has always shown appreciation of the Museum's contribution to local life, and successive mayors have been supportive in different ways. Cllrs Eddie and Mary Waller have held a number of civic receptions at the Priory and in 1992

Gilly Cox (right) giving encouragement to museum organiser (and author of this book) Audrey Ward at the start of an exhibition about fairy tales called Once upon a Time.

A glittering creation given by a member of the Priory staff and modelled by Diana Church, a Priory parent and helper for many years.

created a Mayor's Fund to help towards the restoration of the building. Cllrs Norman and Joan Spiers organised a sparkling Victorian supper to celebrate the opening of the refurbished library in 1993.

From the start, the exhibitions have been constructed and the services of the museum have been run almost entirely by volunteers. We resisted making an admission charge, though we did invite donations. Gifts from the Priory's Parent Teacher Association, from local organisations and local businesses, along with small grants from the Area Museums Service, made it possible to keep the museum running and developing.

For many years the Museum has been fortunate in having regular help with conservation from members of NADFAS, the National Association of Decorative and Fine Arts Societies. They take special care of the large collection of costume and textiles, and over the years they have produced scores of calico dress covers and made the simpler repairs, built up the documentation, and obtained expert advice where necessary. The splendid

costume collection is constantly growing, enabling us from time to time to present parades and displays which arouse great interest and admiration.

Rather than 'curator', I chose the title 'Museum Organiser' (not 'Organist', as I was once addressed) and this title exists to this day. Exhibitions have to be planned and researched, exhibits acquired and displayed, labels and educational material written, posters produced, publicity organised and a launch arranged. The care of the museum collection, the public opening sessions, the reception of visiting groups, the special evening events when we invite experts to lecture at an adult level on our current themes, the conducted tours of the building - all these, and much more, have to be organised.

This mammoth task has been made possible by unstinted help from parents, staff and children, retired people and others with special skills and knowledge. Some started by helping with Museum

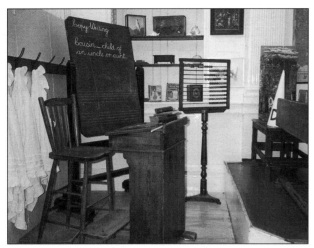

The school section of The Ragged and the Rich, *where visitors could re-live Victorian childhood.*

Museum Organiser Eileen Wood (left) and Emma Currow.

Museum Education Officer, Christina Manners.

Studies - which involved an amount of practical work, some have helped when the museum has been open to the public, and others have specialised in setting up exhibitions. Some have done all three - and some have continued faithfully over most of the Museum's 25 years. A list of names would be very long and I do not trust myself to remember everybody, but I hope that they will all accept this as a tribute and a thank-you. The museum could not exist without them.

New Museum Organisers

In 1992, just as we felt it was time to find a new Museum Organiser, an enquiry came from one of our past Priory pupils, Emma Currow, who had just completed her university degree. We offered her the post, and the school also appointed her to take Museum Studies in the mornings.

For her first year, while the Library was repaired, rewired and redecorated, the Museum could not open to the public, so we worked together on planning and equipping the display area. The new exhibition, entitled *A Somers Dream*, showed how the Library had been used since it had been established by Charles, the third Earl Somers, one hundred and fifty years earlier. In June 1993 there was a grand re-opening, a ceremony most appropriately performed by Anna Somers Cocks.

A month later, the day I retired from responsibility for the day-to-day running of the Museum, could have been a very sad occasion for me, but Gilly Cox had organised a 'goodbye' which was pure Priory Museum Magic. I emerged from the gymnasium following a Priory drama composed and acted by the children - to find all 500 Priory children forming a guard of honour as I was led to a farewell ceremony in the courtyard.

Emma organised two very successful exhibitions, with help from the ever-loyal museum team and a few new helpers from the Friends of the Museum. The first was entitled *What did you do in the war, Mummy?*, and the second, *The Ragged and the Rich*, portrayed these two aspects of Victorian childhood, but she moved to the United States in 1995.

Meanwhile the Museums and Galleries Commission was urging the registration of all museums in order to raise standards and to establish systems which would link up not only British museums, but museums worldwide. For the Priory Museum this entailed a complete reorganisation of the documentation, upgrading of all the storage and conservation arrangements - along with many more time-taking jobs and much form-filling. This is a tremendous task.

We were extremely fortunate that Eileen Wood, who had been increasingly involved over the previous two years, was willing to take over as Museum Organiser, while the school appointed Christina Manners as Museum Education Officer. This arrangement works admirably. Christina shares with the children her growing enthusiasm for the Priory building and its history, and works closely with Eileen Wood and the Priory staff, using the Museum collection to enrich the teaching of topics specified in the National Curriculum.

As Museum Organiser, Eileen Wood uses her own special planning skills, her many talents and her experience of teaching and of business, along with her personal interest in costumes and antiques. Not only is she coping with all the demands for registration, but she has presented, with her hard-working team of artists and scene-builders, three splendid exhibitions, one on the history of shopping, the second, *Happy and Glorious* to commemorate the centenary of Queen Victoria's Diamond Jubilee and now in 1998 the third, showing scenes from Victorian Reigate. To meet the demand for conducted tours of the building she has trained a team of Museum helpers to act as guides.

The Reigate Priory Museum Society

As the 1990s began, great steps forward became possible. We set up a supporters' organisation, 'Friends of Reigate Priory Museum' and in due course this became 'The Reigate Priory Museum Society'. This is a registered charity, with trustees responsible for the Museum's collection of artefacts, and with an executive committee responsible for the running of the Museum. Expert advice was given by the Surrey Museums Development Officer.

The executive committee includes the school head and the Museum Organiser, representatives of the County and Borough Councils, the school staff, governors and parents, the museum volunteers and society members. The museum benefits greatly from the efforts of this committee, which co-ordinates the different functions of the Museum, and spreads awareness of the Priory and of the Museum along many channels.

A termly newsletter is circulated to Society members. Private viewings are held for each new exhibition and a programme of illustrated talks is arranged. There are occasional fund-raising events too. These, along with the members' annual subscriptions and some generous donations from local firms and organisations, mean that the shoestring is no longer so limiting. It has been possible to spend more on mounting exhibitions, and to pay for some clerical help and to install a comprehensive security system. But mainly, the success of the Museum continues to depend upon the devotion of volunteers. There is a great need for more, to share the work, the interesting discoveries and the fun.

Opening times have been extended to two afternoons a week, Wednesdays and Saturdays from 2 to 4.30 p.m. in term-time. There is a growing demand for the museum to open more often, but this would need more volunteers for stewarding duties, and could restrict the school's use of the Holbein Hall. However, a solution could possibly emerge in connection with the restoration project which is envisaged.

The Museum now participates in the nationally organised Heritage Days. Large crowds of visitors from a wide area enjoy talks, additional displays, and conducted tours of the building to illustrate the Priory's history, thus spreading awareness of Reigate Priory to a wider audience.

Future plans

The future holds some exciting possibilities for both the Priory building and the Museum. Perhaps, as a start, information boards could be placed around the house, explaining its history. The Borough and the County are working hard on conservation plans which would include the improvement of the gardens, the preservation of the magnificent wrought iron gates and the restoration, particularly, of the most historic parts of the building.

Surrey County Council's new lease stipulates that they must restore Sir John Parsons' grand staircase and the Verrio murals within the next five years. This will be very costly, so a lottery bid is to be submitted.

The restoration project team stresses the educational and cultural value of having public access while the highly specialised restoration work is in progress and when it is completed. For some years the Museum Committee, under the excellent leadership of Councillor Angela Fraser, has been exploring ways of making an entrance and reception area for the Museum at the west end of the building, to make the Museum more accessible to visitors without causing inconvenience to the school. If the lottery bid succeeds, both projects will be achieved.

During this year, even while this book was being written, there have been many interesting discoveries. One was the archive at the Cambridge Record Office containing Prior Shott's lease with the Priory seal still attached. Another was the discovery by Borough officials of John Parsons' wrought iron gates from the Park Lane entrance. A third is the photograph of Lady Henry Somerset's drawing room before it was extended

in 1895. At Badminton we learned more of the Somerset connection, found family portraits and met Lady Henry's great-grandson. Links are revealed, if we can recognise them, in many unexpected places.

History never stays the same, but grows in two ways. Our knowledge of the past develops with each new discovery, and gradually our pictures of the Priory's history come into sharper focus.

But we are creating history too. The quality of our care of the Priory building, and the way we use it to enrich the lives of people today, are important - for what we do now becomes the history of the future.

As for the discovery of Reigate Priory and its people - it is an ongoing detective story which we can all help to write - and enjoy.

The Museum now participates in the nationally organised Heritage Days. Large crowds of visitors from a wide area enjoy talks, additional displays, and conducted tours of the building to illustrate the Priory's history, thus spreading awareness of Reigate Priory to a wider audience.

BOOKS TO READ AND
PLACES TO VISIT

CHAPTER ONE

Read   *Victorian History of the County of Surrey -*
Part 26, Reigate Hundred (1911), Constable.
The *Cadfael* books by Ellis Peters, Futura.

Visit   Michelham Priory, East Sussex
Mottisfont Abbey, Hampshire
Shrewsbury Abbey and the Shrewsbury Quest
Numerous Augustinian Priory sites owned by English
Heritage.

CHAPTER TWO

Read   *Elizabeth's Admiral, the political career of Charles Howard,*
Earl of Nottingham, 1536 - 1624 by Robert W Kenney,
(1970), Hopkins.

Visit   Reigate Parish Church - Howard memorial.
National Maritime Museum, Greenwich - portraits.
Wilton House, Wilts., Woburn, etc. for portraits of
Elizabeth, Countess of Peterborough.

CHAPTER THREE

Read   *Noted Breweries of Great Britain and Ireland* by A Barnard,
(1889) Causton.
A Brewer's Progress, by L A G Strong (1957).
Handel's Trumpeter, by John Ginger, published by
Pendragon Press 1998.

Visit   St Katherine's Dock area, East London.
Cranston Library, Reigate Parish Church.
Stately homes with Verrio murals, e.g. Burghley,
Chatsworth, Hampton Court.

CHAPTER FOUR

Read   *Diary* of John Evelyn, any edition.

CHAPTER FIVE

Read   *Intelligence Officer in the Peninsula*, by Julia Page (1986),
Spellmount.
England's Michelangelo, a biography of G F Watts, by
Wilfrid Blunt (1975), Hamilton.

Visit   The Watts Gallery at Compton, near Farnham.

CHAPTER SIX

Read   *Lady Henry Somerset*, by Kathleen Fitzpatrick (1923),
Cape.
Beauty for Ashes, by Lady Henry Somerset (1923),
Lupcott Gill and Sons (out of print).

A Victorian Family Portrait, by Brian Hill, Peter Owen.
As We Were, a Victorian Peep-show, by E F Benson (1985),
Hogarth.

Visit   Eastnor Castle and Ledbury.
Brooklands Cemetery.
Churches at Sidlow Bridge and South Park, Reigate.

CHAPTER SEVEN

Read   *The National Trust Country House Album*, by Christopher
Sykes (1989), Pavilion.
Great Hostesses, by B Masters (1982) and paperback
(1989), Constable.

Visit   Polesden Lacey, Surrey (N.T.).
Kedleston Hall, Derbyshire.
Chartwell, Kent (N.T.)

CHAPTER EIGHT

Read   *The Life and Letters of David, Earl Beatty, Admiral of the*
Fleet by Rear-Admiral W S Chalmers (1951) Hodder.
Our Admiral, a biography of Admiral of the Fleet Earl Beatty
by his nephew Charles Beatty (1980) Allen.

Visit   St Paul's Cathedral (memorial).

CHAPTER NINE

Read   *J Arthur Rank, the Man behind the Gong* by Michael
Wakelin, Lion.

See   Videotape *Reigate Priory 1921-48*, by Carolyn Burnley.

Visit   Redhill and Reigate Centre for local and family history
at Redhill Library.

CHAPTERS TEN AND ELEVEN

Visit   REIGATE PRIORY and the MUSEUM. Open
Wednesdays and Saturdays from 2 to 4.30 p.m. in term
time.

FOR GENERAL READING

Malden - *A History of Surrey* (1905) Elliott Stock. Facsimile
(1977), Ep.
Janaway - *Surrey - a County History* (1994) Countryside Books.
R F D Palgrave - *Handbook to Reigate and the Adjoining Parishes*
(1860), reprinted (1973), Kohler and Coombe.
Phillips - *Reigate Guide*, Phillips.
Hooper - *Reigate, its Story through the Ages*, (1943) Surrey
Archaeological Collection, reprinted (1979), Kohler.
Scears - *A History of Reigate Priory* (out of print).

INDEX